START
STITCHING

© 2014 by New Design Originals Corporation, www.d-originals.com, an imprint of Fox Chapel Publishing, 800-457-9112, 1970 Broad Street, East Petersburg, PA 17520.

Library of Congress Cataloging-in-Publication Data

Love stitching
  Start stitching / editors of Future publishing.
     pages cm
  Summary: "Presents information on how to sew many types of stitches as well as techniques for embellishing stitched items. Introduces the skills and techniques through a variety of inspirational projects and step-by-step instructions"-- Provided by publisher.
  "First published in 2013 in the United Kingdom by Future Publishing Limited in magazine form under the title Love Stitching."
  ISBN 978-1-57421-730-8 (paperback)
  1. Needlework. 2. Stitches (Sewing) I. Title.
  TT750.L67 2014
  746.44--dc23
                          2013044747

Printed in China
First printing

START
STITCHING

SWEET AND SIMPLE PROJECTS FOR NEEDLE & THREAD

Design Originals

an Imprint of Fox Chapel Publishing

www.d-originals.com

Ready to Stitch?

HAND-STITCHED ITEMS are everywhere at the moment, and it's time for you to join in! In this book you'll find a variety of inspirational projects introducing you to a new technique every time. Whether it's a beautiful cushion, purse, wall hanging, party bag or greeting card, you'll love showing off your new skills.

The first part of this book focuses on the stitches, introducing you to long stitch, blackwork, cross stitch, French knots and much more – all traditional stitches that have gained fresh appeal for contemporary crafters. Then, you'll learn techniques for embellishing your stitched items, including appliqué, beading, ribbons, buttons and other fun ideas. So let's get started!

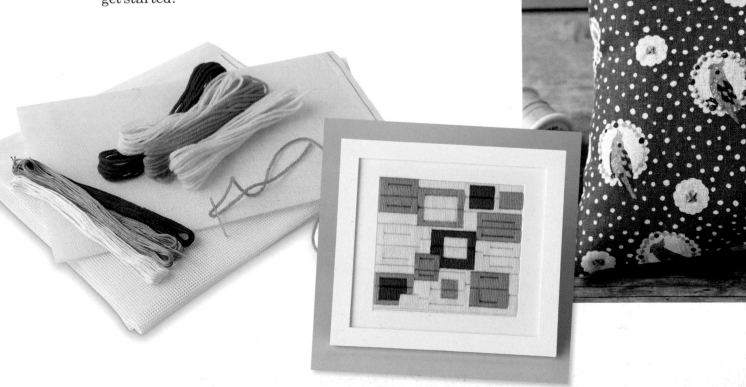

START STITCHING

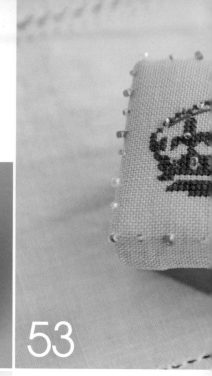

31

53

58

36

stitching basics

projects

Stitching
basics

The art of creating beautiful
patterns in fabric and thread is
easy enough for anyone to do!
Here's your guide through
the basics…

INSERT NEEDLE
THROUGH GUIDE HOLE
TO ALIGN
THE TWO PARTS

ROLLED EDGES   SIZE   RECESSED SEWING
PREVENT   2   HOLES ENSURE
CUTTING THREAD   PERFECT CLOSING

MADE IN ENGLAND

Essential sewing supplies

If you're new to stitching and sewing, there are a few essential items you'll need to stock up on – assemble your supplies using our list below.

1 THREADS
There's a thread for almost every occasion and your local craft store can help you find the right one for your project. Many embroidery projects use embroidery floss, which is a great all-purpose thread. With embroidery floss, each thread length is made up of six strands of cotton twisted together. Most embroidery stitches are made using one or two strands of floss, but the project instructions should indicate how many strands to use when stitching different parts of your design. See page 11 for more details about threads.

2 BUTTONS
Buttons can be used for practical reasons, to secure the back of a cushion cover for instance, or just for decoration, to add texture and variety to your work.

3 FASTENINGS
Safety pins can hold fabrics together when ordinary pins may fall out. Snap fasteners and other fastenings, such as hooks and eyes, may also be useful.

4 SEAM RIPPER
If you're upcycling vintage fabrics or clothing, there are some occasions when you need this handy gadget to help your undoing go smoothly and quickly.

5 THIMBLE
If you're regularly stitching or working with thicker fabrics, a thimble will save you from pricking your finger.

6 EMBROIDERY SCISSORS
At about 5" (13cm) long, these are much smaller than fabric scissors. The fine, straight blade makes them good for trimming stray threads.

7 NEEDLES
You can get specialist needles for embroidery and appliqué, but it's also handy to have a pack of assorted general-purpose sewing needles. For basic embroidery stitches, you'll need an embroidery or crewel needle with a sharp tip, which is ideal for fine details such as backstitch and French knots.

8 THREAD CUTTER
These are great for when you're traveling or you don't have space for scissors. If you plan to take an embroidery project on a flight, check the airline's restrictions.

9 FABRIC
There's a huge range of different fabrics available, so your choice is almost limitless! Embroidery projects can be completed on almost any fabric, but always check the project instructions for advice on which sort of fabric to use. If you're after a specific amount of fabric, you'll find it's usually sold by the yard or meter. However, some fabrics are sold in 'fat quarters', which are pieces measuring about 18"x22" (45.5x56cm).

10 PINS
Use these to hold pieces of fabric together. Regular dressmakers' pins can be tricky, so try pins with larger heads– these lie flat so you can iron over them.

11 FABRIC SCISSORS
Keep your fabric scissors sharp by only using them for fabric. Look for some that are about 8" (20cm) long and have a curved handle to enable accurate

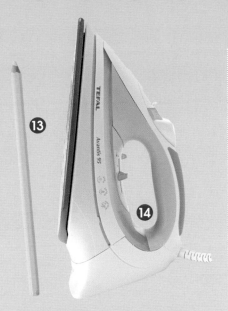

⑬

⑭

cutting on flat surfaces, with pointed tips for precision.

12 TAPE MEASURE
Measuring your fabric correctly is one of the essential elements of creating a perfect embroidery design (measure twice, cut once!), so make sure you buy a tape measure that's at least 60" (150cm) long and has both metric and imperial units for quick conversions. Some have different colored sections to make measuring even easier.

13 FABRIC PENCIL
A fabric pencil is essential for tracing embroidery designs onto your fabric. They come in different shades, so you can find the color that stands out best on your material. You could also try a chalk pencil with a brush for erasing unwanted lines, or water-soluble pens and pencils that will disappear when you dampen or wash the fabric.

14 IRON
Crumpled fabrics can cause stitching mishaps, so you'll usually need to press your material before you start stitching. An iron is also useful for attaching appliqué shapes using fusible webbing. Use an ironing cloth or a tea towel to protect delicate fabrics when you iron them, and only iron on the reverse side.

Know your threads

Embroidery flosses are the most popular threads for embroidery but there are plenty of other options…

Madeira Lana
Create fluffy creatures to your heart's content with Madeira Lana thread. Stitch as you would with ordinary embroidery floss. When you've finished, use the rough side of a piece of hook and loop tape to fluff up the stitches. Keep going until you're happy with the texture.

Multicolor thread
For a unique, color-changing effect without any extra work, try out Anchor Multicolor thread. It's great for stitching flowers, lettering or any large block of color.

Linen
DMC Linen has a matte finish and comes in beautiful muted tones. It's perfect for any vintage-inspired projects. Remove the L from the color code to find the same color in normal embroidery floss.

Satin

Add a glamorous sheen to your stitching with DMC Satin threads. Each color has an embroidery floss equivalent, so they're simple to mix and match in any project that needs an extra special touch.

Hand dyed

For rich, vibrant hues, nothing beats hand-dyed thread, like the Sassy Strings range from Sassy's Fabbys. Be careful though, because hand-dyed threads aren't always colorfast.

Floche
Cotton floche is one of the highest quality embroidery threads out there. It has a high luster and is much softer than traditional embroidery floss.

Fluorescent
When you really need your stitching to stand out, use DMC Fluorescent Effects threads. Try stitching a motif on black fabric for the ultimate color contrast!

Glow in the dark

This unassuming white thread from DMC glows green in the dark, making it perfect for leaving secret pictures and messages in your design that will only be seen once the lights go out. Kids will love it!

Pearl cotton

DMC Pearl cotton is a twisted thread, making it thicker than embroidery floss. Use just one strand instead of two to give your design a textured effect. It works well for free-hand embroidery and backstitch lettering.

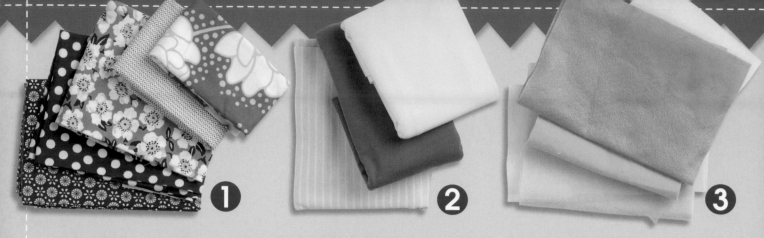

All about fabric

There are hundreds of fabrics out there, so learn to understand your options and pick the perfect material for every project.

WOVEN FABRICS ❶

Take a close look at a woven fabric and you'll see that it's made from two groups of threads, a warp (the threads that run lengthwise) and a weft (the threads that run widthwise). It will also have a border called a selvage, which is more tightly woven to prevent the fabric from unraveling (don't use this in your stitching). Cotton is one of the world's most popular woven fabrics. It's strong, easy to work with and can be washed at high temperatures. However, it wrinkles easily, so it's often blended with other fibers. Linen, woven from flax fibers, is even stronger than cotton, although it also has a tendency to crease.

NON-WOVEN FABRICS ❷

Unlike the straight warp and weft of woven materials, knitted fabrics use loops of yarn running in rows or columns. These fabrics are much more flexible and stretchy than woven cloth. You can easily embroider onto these fabrics but beware that the area you stitch onto won't stretch as much afterwards. It's also essential to use a hoop on stretchy fabrics, for an even tension. Many non-woven fabrics are created by compressing individual fibers into a solid mass. One example of this is interfacing, which is a type of fabric that provides an extra layer of support to your material and stiffens it. Choose an interfacing that's slightly lighter than your fabric, and if you're using a fusible (iron-on) option then always test it on a scrap of the fabric. Make sure you attach it to the fabric before adding your embroidery.

FELT, NET AND LACE ❸

Felt is created by condensing woolen fibers, either using a machine or by hand in soapy water. You can also felt knitted fabric by putting it in a washing machine at a high temperature. This fabric is particularly popular with crafters and embroidery beginners because it's fray-resistant, doesn't stretch like woven materials and can easily be cut to any shape. Net and lace are fabrics created without compressing, weaving or knitting – both of these are made by knotting together lengths of thread to create a pattern. These materials are often used as decoration, and are best cut with small, sharp scissors for a neat finish. Always check what your fabric is made from before you wash it, in case of shrinkage.

GO SHOPPING

Collecting fabrics for your stash is fun, but if you have a particular project in mind then it's best not to impulse buy! Make sure you know what to look for before leaving the house. Your shopping list should include the type of fabric, the exact amount you need and any colors or prints you think would go well with the design. Always buy your threads at the same time as your fabric – this way it's easier to make sure that the colors match exactly. If possible, take the pattern with you, because your local fabric store will be able to offer advice if you are not sure what you need.

STANDARD FABRIC WIDTHS

Fabrics are sold in standard widths, which vary according to their purpose– for example, voile material for curtains is usually a different width than dressmakers' cotton cloth, which generally comes in standard widths of 36" (90cm) or 45" (115cm). However, some manufacturers use metric units and some use imperial, so a fabric measuring 36" will actually be a bit wider than 90cm. If this could make a difference to your project then it's recommended to bring a tape measure and check the figures for yourself. You will also see 'fat quarters' for sale. This is a quarter of a yard or meter of fabric, produced by cutting half a yard of fabric in half across the length. This gives you a piece of fabric about 18"x22" or 45.5x56cm. Always double check you're buying the right amount of fabric.

mix & match

If you're new to embroidery, it's best to start off using plain colors rather than patterned fabrics. A plain block of color, especially in muted shades, will suit most designs and make sure your stitching is the part that stands out. Once you're more confident with embroidery and color, look around at some of the beautiful patterned fabrics available. Some fabrics with subtle patterns can look great with areas of embroidery!

Using templates

Most embroidery projects use templates, which you'll need to transfer onto your fabric to recreate the design. Here's how…

1 Before you start tracing, make sure your fabric is wrinkle free. Plan carefully where you want to place the design and make sure you leave yourself enough space. Check the project instructions for details of whether you need to enlarge your template on a photocopier. You can enlarge or reduce any design to suit your specific project.

2 The simplest way to transfer a design onto your fabric is to trace it. Hold the fabric right side up and place it over the template. Secure with masking tape so that it can't slip. Trace over all the lines using a pencil. If you struggle to see the design through the fabric, trace the design onto tracing paper using a fine black pen. Then tape the design and fabric to a window or a light box, and trace the design. To help with this, you could turn your fabric upside down and stretch it into a hoop or frame so that the right side of the fabric is in the back of the hoop and the wrong side is flush against the design surface. Make sure the template is easy to see and draw around it using a fabric pencil. Finally, remove the fabric from your frame and reinsert it right side up, ready to embroider.

3 If your fabric is too thick to do this or it's impossible to trace through the window, trace the design onto tracing paper and secure to your fabric with pins. Following your pencil lines, tack around the design using small, even stitches in a contrasting colored thread. Score along your tacking stitches with the tip of a needle and then remove the paper by simply tearing, and you're ready to go.

4 Alternatively, try dressmakers' carbon paper. First, trace the design onto plain paper. Cut a piece of dressmakers' carbon paper to fit the size of the design. Place the carbon paper over your fabric, where you want to place the design, with the dark side next to the fabric surface. Place your paper template on top and trace over the outline using a blunt pencil or similar. Remove the

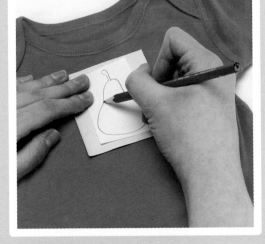

carbon paper and you will have created a dark outline for your embroidery design.

5 Once you've drawn your design onto the fabric, place it into a hoop. This will provide the correct tension, your stitches will be neater and it will prevent the fabric from puckering. If you're right-handed, work the embroidery stitches from right to left – if you're left-handed, work from left to right instead.

TRACE your picture directly onto your fabric using a washable or fading fabric pen, available at most craft and sewing shops.
PLACE dressmaker's carbon paper face down onto your fabric. Place your picture on top and trace using a blunt pencil.

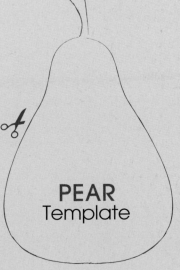

PEAR
Template

Using a sewing machine

Get all the know-how on using a sewing machine so you can finish your stitched creations in style!

W hether you're a machine novice or just need a refresher, here's a guide to finding your way around a sewing machine. Every machine varies slightly, so some of these functions might work differently, or yours might have extra features. Refer to your manual for exactly how to use your machine.

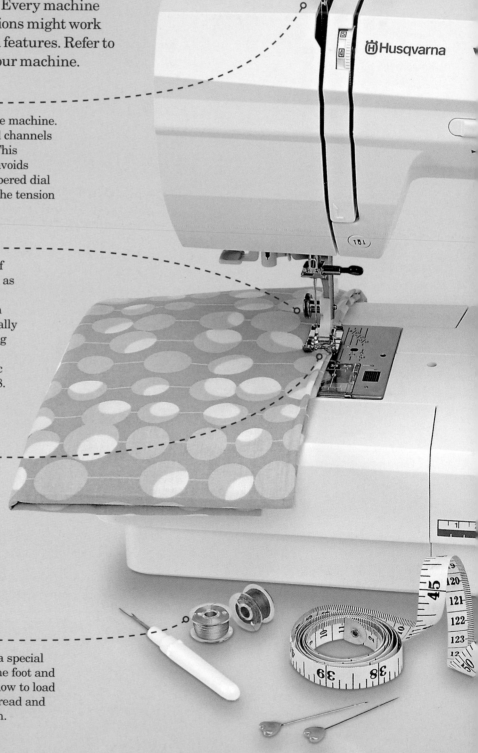

THREAD FEED
Your spool of thread sits at the top of the machine. It threads through a series of numbered channels and loops before it reaches the needle. This maintains an even thread tension and avoids tangles. Your machine will have a numbered dial that can be raised or lowered to adjust the tension as your fabric requires.

NEEDLE
A sewing machine needle moves in and out of the fabric without going all the way through, as in hand sewing. Most machines come with a needle in place, but your manual will explain how to change it. Standard needles are typically size 11 or 12. For tougher jobs, such as sewing denim or very heavy curtains, go for a larger number – 18 or 19. When sewing a fine fabric such as organza or sheer net, use a fine size 8. When you buy your fabric, it's worth asking which needle is best for the job.

FOOT
This is the metal attachment that sits beneath your needle and holds your fabric in place. There's a lever to move it up and down. Raise it up when positioning your fabric and move it down when sewing. The foot works with the feed dogs underneath the fabric to hold it in place. Your machine should come with a basic presser foot, but there are dozens of speciality feet, including a darning foot for machine embroidery.

BOBBIN
This small plastic or metal spool sits in a special housing under the sewing area, below the foot and needle. Check your manual for exactly how to load your bobbin. Once loaded, the bobbin thread and top thread feeds meet to form each stitch.

STITCH SELECTOR

Dials, switches, knobs… the method used to change the stitch type varies between machines, but the principle is the same. You'll mostly use the basic straight stitch and zigzag, but once you're more confident, try some of the more decorative stitches your machine has to offer.

HAND WHEEL

Use the hand wheel to move the needle up and down manually, to control the sewing line in tight spots and corners. To avoid getting tangled threads, always turn the wheel toward you. To wind bobbins, you'll need to disengage the needle action by pulling out this wheel or pressing a switch. Check your manual for how to do this on your machine.

STITCH WIDTH

Sometimes this function is built in, so the machine automatically adjusts this as you change the stitch type. If your machine has a width dial, leave it at 0 for straight stitches because the needle doesn't need to move from side to side. For other stitches, simply adjust the width as needed, practicing on a scrap of fabric first.

STITCH LENGTH

A dial or knob will enable you to change the length of your stitches, whether they're simple straight stitches, zigzags or any other pattern. A long stitch length is useful for creating quick tacking lines. For regular stitching, aim for a length of around 2 or 2.5, but experiment with the stitch length and practice on a fabric scrap.

REVERSE STITCHING

Most machines have a button or switch to enable you to sew in the reverse direction. Even older machines should have a method for reverse stitching – it's handy for embroidering various shapes. Stitching forwards and backwards for an inch or so will also secure your threads at the start and end of your stitching.

FOOT PEDAL

The foot pedal is connected to the machine and sits on the floor. The pedal is pressure-sensitive, so gentle pressure results in slow stitching, while pressing harder will run the motor faster. Some machines also have a separate speed control, which gives you even more command over your pace.

Start Stitching

Machine stitches

Learn how to use your sewing machine to work all sorts of machine embroidery stitches, techniques and styles...

Getting started

Start off by doodling and playing with the different stitches on your sewing machine. Play with straight stitches, in different lengths and colors, then move on to zigzag stitches in different sizes and types. Then try making scribbles and loops. Just have fun!

Make shapes

Move on to making basic outlines for various shapes, such as circles, squares, hearts and flowers. Practice making double outlines by going around the shape again – your aim should be to get the shapes tidy but still sketchy.

Start shading

Once you're confident making outlines, try coloring them in, which is called shading. Move the fabric backwards and forwards to fill the outline with stitches of thread, a bit like satin stitch in hand embroidery.

Appliqué motifs

Add an extra dimension to your shapes with appliqué. Cut out shaped pieces of fabric and attach with straight stitch or zigzag stitch outlines, or try stitching over both the appliqué shape and the background fabric.

Make sure your background and appliqué fabrics work together, then play with different stitch styles to find the best way to attach them

Layered appliqué

Put together all the skills you've practiced and you can create gorgeous designs like this present – it's layered up with appliqué motifs, outlining, shading and other interesting stitch styles.

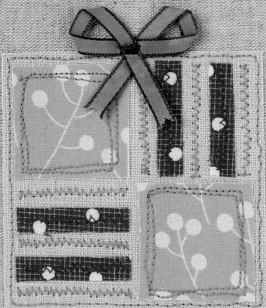

Stitching

Follow these projects to get to grips with
some fabulous stitches

All in the detail ♡

Textured stitching

YOU WILL NEED

☐ Embroidery linen (5¼"x8" (13x20cm))

☐ Neutral, striped fabric

☐ Embroidery floss and Madeira Lana thread

☐ Vintage buttons

☐ General sewing supplies, including scissors, pins, washable fabric marker, etc.

Give your projects a little extra detail, from French knots and couching to fluffy Lana thread

Simple projects can be made all the more interesting with the addition of a little detail. In the next few pages, you'll learn how to create texture on a project using three easy techniques. Use French knots to create a cute berry button for a card, try couching to embellish a cushion and distress special Lana threads for a fluffy look.

These are great projects to try if you're new to stitching. Find an old purse or cushion and add your own details to give it a makeover. Once you've tried these techniques you'll be ready to make one of the gorgeous projects featured here.

Give your projects some lift!

These are great projects to try if you're new to stitching. Find an old purse or cushion cover and give it a makeover

Go baaa-rmy for French knots to create this cute sheep scene...

NEEDLE WALLET

To make this sweet book for storing needles and pins, trace the lettering on to the right side of a 5¼"x8" (13x20cm) piece of linen. Use couching for 'Pins &' and regular backstitch for 'Needles'. With right sides in, back your stitching with striped fabric and sew around the outside. Turn right sides out and slip stitch closed. Add a piece of felt to the inside, stitching through the center of your book to secure. Finish with vintage buttons.

DANDELION NOTEBOOK

Work your dandelion heads (template on page 25) using three strands of Lana. Fluff up, then add short straight stitches around the outside. Attach the stems with couching stitches. Use vertical stitches for the grass.

TRY...COUCHING
This technique was made famous by the Bayeux Tapestry

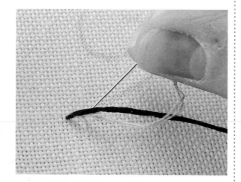

1 Bring your base thread (dark red) up to the front of your fabric. Bring your couching thread (lime) up to the front, just to the side of your base thread, then come back down again on the other side of the base thread.

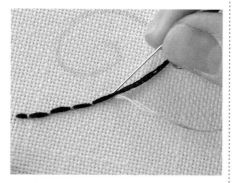

2 You can choose a coordinating thread or go for a contrasting color, as shown here. Continue adding the couching stitches at regular intervals – every few millimeters along the length of your design.

WORK WITH...LANA THREAD
This textured yarn has a lovely furry feel when fluffed up

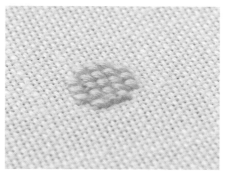

1 Whenever you work on a project which combines Madeira Lana thread and other types of embroidery, always work the Lana areas first. Stitch just as you would with embroidery floss, using two or three strands of Lana.

2 Use a rough piece of hook and loop tape to fluff up the stitched threads. Lightly stroke the Lana until it becomes fluffy, being careful not to stroke it too hard. Once you're happy with the results, finish stitching the rest of your design.

TOP TIP
Why not try the couching stitch using a thick, luxurious yarn or rustic twine with invisible thread (or fishing wire)? The finished result is a strip with a lovely textured effect which still allows your gorgeous yarn to stand out.

SHEEP STITCH HOOP
Work the face and legs of your sheep first, filling in with straight stitches. Fill in the gate posts with cross stitches and the horizontal bars with long straight stitches. Finish with hundreds and hundreds of French knots! Turn the page to see how to get started...

Simple projects can be made all the more interesting with the addition of a little detail

TWINE HEART SACHET
This rustic sachet couldn't be easier. Draw a heart shape on your fabric. Try using the couching technique to create the twine heart. Finish with a wooden button in the center.

BERRY BUTTON CARD

This bijoux berry is the perfect starting point if you'd like to build up your French knot confidence. Stitch onto a small piece of linen. Once you've finished, wrap around a 1¼" (29mm) self-cover button.

MAKE...FRENCH KNOTS

If at first you don't succeed, try and try again

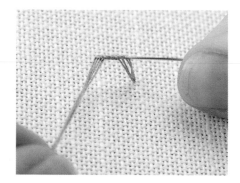

1 Use a sharp needle, which will help pierce the fabric. Bring your needle up at your starting point and wrap your thread once or twice around the needle. Here four strands of floss are used, but the choice is yours.

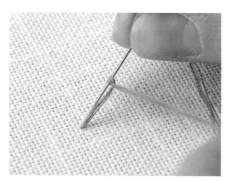

2 Hold your thread end firmly and take your needle down, ever so slightly over from where you came up. This helps secure the knot and prevent it from escaping through the same hole!

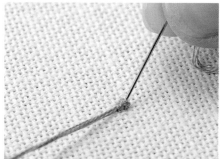

3 Slide the twisted thread down the needle so that it rests on the fabric's surface, and gently feed the needle through the fabric. Keep your thread as taut as possible to keep the knot secure.

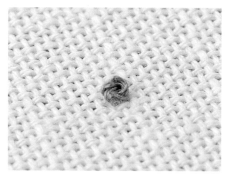

4 Gently pull your thread through to tighten the knot, so that it sits neatly on the surface and looks rounded as shown. If you tighten the knot too much it will disappear, so practice on spare fabric until you're more confident.

TEMPLATES FOR YOUR TEXTURED PROJECTS

Pins

&

Needles

PINS & NEEDLES BOOK

SHEEP STITCH HOOP

BERRY BUTTON CARD

TEMPLATE TRANSFER

The easiest way to transfer the above templates onto your fabric is to photocopy this page and tape it to a window. Use a fading fabric pen to trace the shape onto your fabric. If you don't have a fabric pen a pencil will do, just be sure to completely cover the lines with stitches.

MADEIRA LANA

This thread is tricky to find in the US, but you can order it online at *www.barnyarns.co.uk*. Its blend of materials makes it unique to work with, but you can also try achieving the fluffy effect described on page 22 by using No. 3 pearl cotton thread instead.

DANDELION CHART

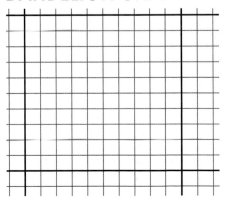

Pattern perfection
Sashiko embroidery

This beautiful Japanese embroidery technique creates simple yet elegant geometric patterns.

YOU WILL NEED

☐ Dark blue or gray linen or linen blend fabric with a medium weave (big enough for a cushion)

☐ White or navy Sashiko thread (or thick embroidery thread)

☐ Sashiko needle (very sharp and long)

☐ Dressmaker's carbon paper or washable fabric pen

☐ General sewing supplies, including scissors, pins, washable fabric marker, etc.

Sashiko, or 'little stabs', originates from 18th-century rural Japan. This running stitch technique was first used to sew patches onto worn or torn clothing. And though it has developed into a purely decorative art, it still remains tied to its roots. The designs are predominantly geometric, each carrying a specific meaning. The traditional color scheme is white thread on dark blue fabric, though countless variations can be seen in contemporary Sashiko – do a search on Pinterest for a gorgeous gallery of inspiration!

Start with these simple cushion and card projects to enter the world of Sashiko...

Shaping up to be pretty!

Sashiko designs are geometric, each with a specific meaning. The traditional color scheme is white thread on dark blue fabric

Sashiko looks very stylish but is simply a running stitch around a design.

CUSHION
This traditional geometric design is the perfect starting point for beginners. Once you've finished stitching, any remaining guidelines can be carefully removed with a bit of water. Once dry, press flat and transform into a cushion, wall hanging or whatever else you would like to make.

HOW TO... SASHIKO EMBROIDERY

Get started in Sashiko with this handy step-by-step guide

HOW TO... TRANSFER PATTERNS

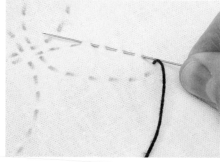

FOR DARK FABRICS

1 Make a quilter's knot by wrapping your thread around your needle twice. Pinch the wrapped thread and pull down to form the knot. Come up to the front of the fabric with your needle.

2 Instead of working each stitch individually, work back and forth through the fabric without pulling all the way through. Once you have several stitches on your needle, gently pull through.

Place a piece of white dressmaker's carbon paper facedown on your fabric. Place your pattern on top and trace using a pencil. Remove the carbon paper to reveal your design.

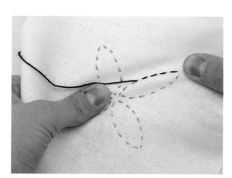

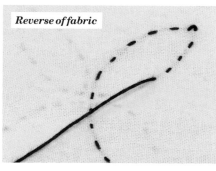

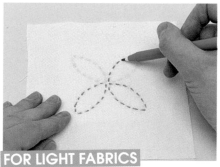

Reverse of fabric

FOR LIGHT FABRICS

3 Next, pull your fabric taut to reduce puckering. Your stitches should be slightly longer on the front than on the back. Continue, working as many stitches at one time as you feel comfortable with.

4 If you come to a corner or change direction in the pattern, leave a bit of slack on the reverse to allow for puckering. Once you've finished your length of thread, finish with a second quilter's knot to secure.

Trace your picture directly onto your fabric using a washable or fading fabric pen. Once you've finished stitching, spray with water to remove your guidelines.

CARD

For a quick and easy introduction into the world of Sashiko, this card is just right. Cut your finished stitching into a patch and fray the outer rows of linen. For a perfect finish, back with fusible webbing, then adhere to a simple white card.

PINCUSHION

Can you see flowers within the larger circular design? This is the beauty of Sashiko patterns. Create your pincushion just as you would a larger cushion, though you'll want to stuff it a bit more firmly to hold the pins in place.

TOP TIP

Why not adapt this pincushion idea into hanging Christmas decorations? Make round cushions with the circular Sashiko design on the front using festive color fabrics and threads.

MATERIALS

FABRIC
You'll want a linen or linen blend fabric with a medium weave. If the weave is too tight it will pucker.

THIMBLE
Though not an essential, you may find it more comfortable to stitch using this speciality thimble to help you push the needle through your fabric.

THREADS
Sashiko thread is thicker than embroidery thread and is non-divisible. It has a matte finish and is available in single color or variegated varieties.

NEEDLES
Sashiko needles are long with a sharp point and small eye. This is to allow for working several stitches at once.

TEMPLATES FOR SASHIKO STITCHING

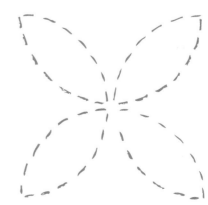

You can use a photocopier to enlarge your patterns to whatever size you like

Going the distance
Long stitch

This striking, beautifully-textured technique can be used to create all kinds of stunning effects

Everything you need to know about this stitch is in the name! Long stitch is a form of needlepoint that involves combining stitches in a variety of lengths to create an image or pattern. The stitches are traditionally vertical, but the possibilities for variations are endless. Turn the page to find out how to create interesting effects with your long stitch designs, such as the quilted style used for the featured geometric picture. Plus, you can put your skill to good use and learn how to create your own unique long stitch pattern.

Gorgeously soft stitches

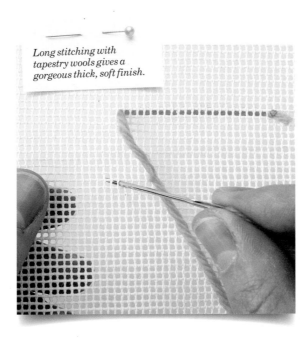

Long stitching with tapestry wools gives a gorgeous thick, soft finish.

The stitches are traditionally vertical, but the possibilities for variations are endless

This geometric picture has been worked using tapestry wools on 14 count interlock canvas. As long as you stick to simple geometric shapes, you can create your own patterns.

HOW TO... LONG STITCH

Get started with this handy step-by-step stitching guide

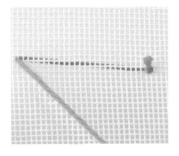

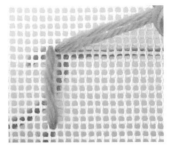

1 Thread your needle and knot the end of your wool. Take your needle down through the front of your fabric. Come back up an inch or two over from your knot. As you stitch, work over the starting thread to secure.

2 Complete your first stitch by coming back down again, creating a vertical line. Avoid making your stitches too long, or they will appear loose and the canvas will show through. Break up long lines with the 'Quilted' effect.

3 For your next stitch, come up next to where you came up for your previous stitch, NOT next to where you took your thread back down. This way, more wool will be left on the back of the canvas, making your design sturdier.

4 Continue until you've stitched over your starting thread several times, then snip the knot. Once you've finished your thread length, secure by weaving your thread through the backs of your stitches.

HOW TO DO... VARIOUS TECHNIQUES

Once you've mastered the basics there are plenty of techniques to try

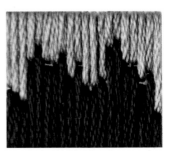

QUILTED

Draw a horizontal line through your square, then fill in the shape using broken vertical lines. This is great for breaking up shapes that are too tall to work in single lines.

VARIED LENGTHS

Create the visual effect of a mountain range by stitching your first color in descending and ascending stitch lengths, then fill in with your second color.

LONG AND SHORT

Work a row of stitches of the same length, leaving an empty row between each. Work your next row halfway up the length of the first and so on for each new row.

EMBROIDERY FLOSS

For a more delicate, shiny finish, work your design using six strands of floss on size 24 canvas. Anything you see worked in wool will also work in embroidery floss.

NEEDLEBOOK

Although canvas is very stiff, it doesn't mean you can't sew your creations into usable items. Here, take part of the design and work it into the front of a needlebook.

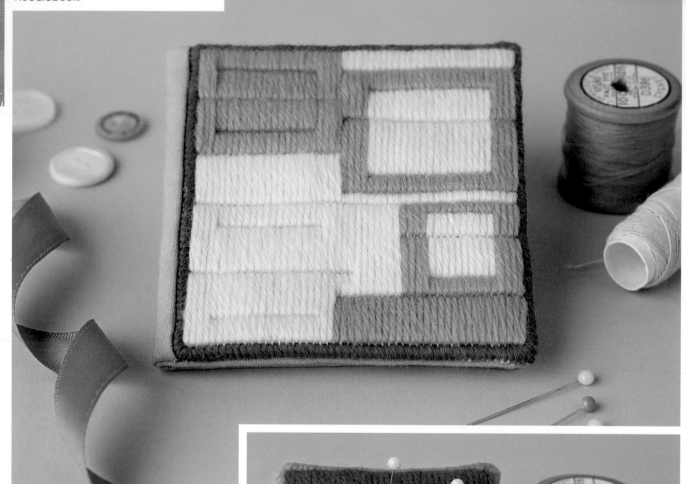

TOP TIP
Threading your needle
To thread your needle with tapestry wool, fold your thread end around the eye of the needle and pinch. Take this pinched loop and slide through the eye.

Any of the examples you see that are worked in tapestry wool will also work in embroidery floss

PINCUSHION

A contrasting orange border really helps the blue tones pop in this simple yet effective design, which mimics a mountain range. You could also try using the same technique to create a cityscape.

MATERIALS

TAPESTRY WOOLS

Tapestry wools are 4-ply and non-divisible. Stitch using just one strand in your needle. Anchor, DMC and Appleton are all high quality brands.

CANVAS

These tapestry wool designs are worked with 14 count interlock canvas. If you're using embroidery flosses, use 24 count canvas.

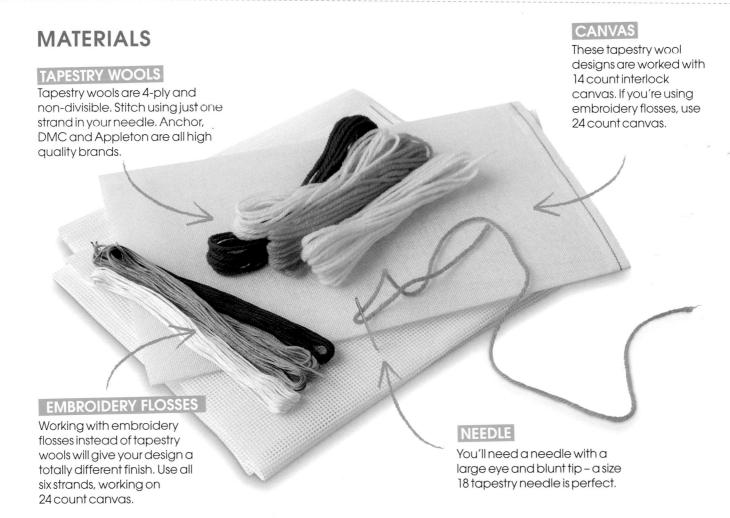

EMBROIDERY FLOSSES

Working with embroidery flosses instead of tapestry wools will give your design a totally different finish. Use all six strands, working on 24 count canvas.

NEEDLE

You'll need a needle with a large eye and blunt tip – a size 18 tapestry needle is perfect.

CREATING YOUR PATTERN

To create your own unique long stitch pattern, get out your colored paper and scissors and begin cutting out squares and rectangles in a variety of sizes. Layer them up until you're happy with the finished look, then cover the whole thing in transparent adhesive tape. Lay your canvas over the top of your design and simply trace the shapes with pencil to transfer the pattern. Draw a horizontal line through each square to break up long lines and create a quilted effect.

Loved up! ♡
Cross stitch

These cards make a great alternative to the classic Valentine's greetings, and are super simple to stitch and make

Cross stitching is one of the easiest techniques to master and it's incredibly addictive too! With just a few simple stitches you'll soon be making cute projects to give away as gifts. Here, you can try a contemporary card idea for loved ones suitable for Valentine's Day or any other time you want to show you care!

.

Cute and clever card idea!

Cross stitch is a great technique for producing bold, colorful motifs with ease

New to cross stitch? Turn the page and get started with your new favorite hobby!

PATCH CARDS

Press your stitching flat on the reverse. Trim into a patch and fray the outer row of aida blocks all the way around. Back your stitching with a piece of white card using double-sided tape. Cut a piece of card to 5½"x8¼" (14x21cm) and fold in half. Attach your stitching to the front of the card using 3D foam pads.

Your stitching tension varies naturally from day to day, and it's more noticeable when working solid blocks of color. Keep these areas looking flat by finishing each stitching session at the end of a row

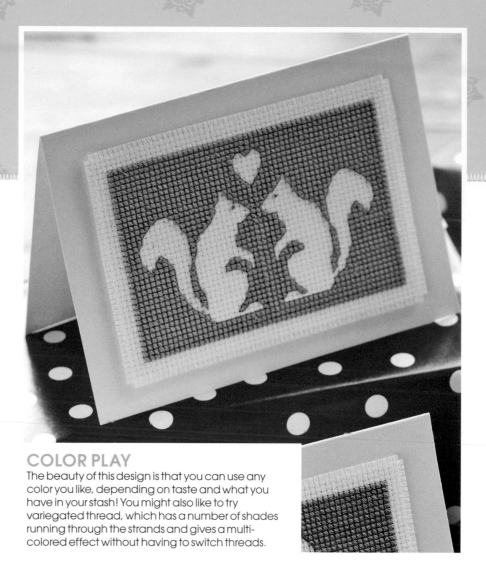

COLOR PLAY

The beauty of this design is that you can use any color you like, depending on taste and what you have in your stash! You might also like to try variegated thread, which has a number of shades running through the strands and gives a multi-colored effect without having to switch threads.

HOW TO... START STITCHING

This clever waste knot keeps the back neat

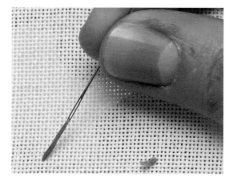 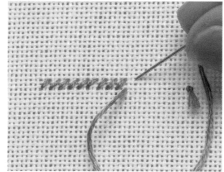 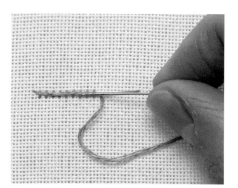

1 Knot one end of your thread and take it down through the front of your fabric, about ¾" (2cm) from your starting point. Then bring it back up to the front of your fabric to make your first stitch.

2 Begin stitching your design, making sure you're stitching over your starting thread with each stitch. You can work whole stitches or work half stitches and then come back.

3 Once you're happy that your starting thread is secure, snip off the knot. To secure your thread when you've finished stitching, weave it through the backs of your stitches as shown here.

HOW TO... CROSS STITCH ON AIDA
Get started and before you know it you'll be an expert!

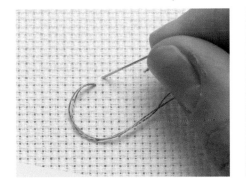

1 Cut a 16" (40cm) thread length and thread your needle with the number of strands instructed by the key. Make a waste knot (see previous page). Make a diagonal half cross stitch across a single aida block (or across two blocks if you choose to stitch on evenweave or linen).

2 Make a second diagonal stitch to complete your first cross. Alternatively, you can work a row of half cross stitches first, then work back to complete the stitches. The is often quicker when covering large areas in a single color.

3 The direction of your diagonals is up to you; just be sure all your stitches cross in the same direction. Otherwise, your design will look uneven. Continue working from the center outward.

HOW TO... CROSS STITCH FRACTIONALS
These little stitches really help your design take shape

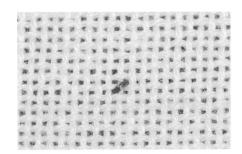

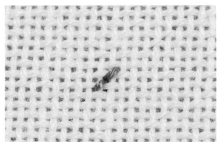

1 Start with a quarter stitch, working from one corner into the center. With aida, you'll need to pierce the center of the block. For evenweave, there is already a hole in the center to stitch into.

2 Make your next quarter stitch in your second color, coming up from the opposite corner and back down through the center. You've now created a half cross stitch.

3 Finish your stitch by making a half cross stitch. Fractionals are shown in the chart either as two symbols opposite one another in a chart square, or by a symbol opposite an empty space.

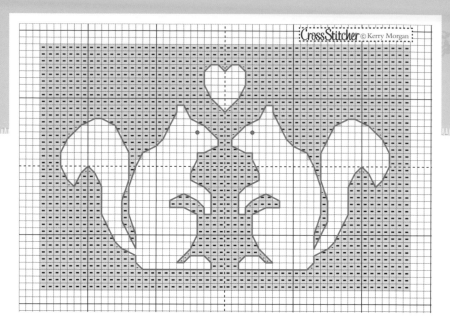

CHARTS
FOR YOUR PROJECTS

*Use the colors listed here, or
choose some from your stash!*

	DMC	Anchor	Madeira
Cross stitch in three strands			
▬	703	238	1307
★	3608	086	0709
♥	3801	1098	0411
Backstitch in one strand			
—	349	013	0212
	birds and heart		
—	702	226	1306
	squirrels and heart		
—	3607	087	0708
	penguins and heart		
French knots in one strand			
(see page 24 for the technique)			
●	349	013	0212
	bird eyes		
●	702	226	1306
	squirrel eyes		
●	3607	087	0708
	penguin eyes		

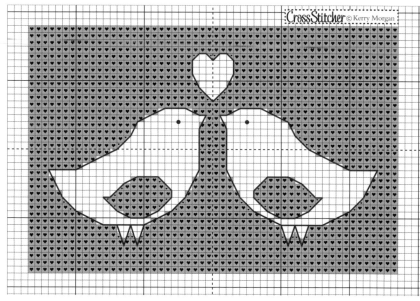

HOW TO... BACK STITCH
*Work backstitch with a sharp needle once all the cross
stitch is complete.*

1 Work the backstitch over about 1-3
chart squares at a time, making sure
to closely follow the chart. Any longer
and your stitches could end up becoming
loose and pulling out.

2 For each additional stitch, bring your
needle up 1-3 chart squares away from
your previous stitch. Then pass it back
through the fabric at the same point as
your previous stitch. To secure your thread,
weave it through the back of your stitches,
then bring your needle up to the surface.

HOW TO...
USE THE CHARTS
It's easy when you know how...

WHERE TO START

Start stitching from the center of the design and your fabric. The center of these charts are indicated by dotted lines. To find the center of your fabric, fold it in half and then into quarters.

Each square on the chart represents a single cross stitch. Fractionals are half filled squares or squares filled with two different colors.

THE KEY AND SYMBOLS

All the symbols that appear on the chart are listed in the key with their corresponding thread codes beside them. The key also tells you the different stitches used in the design.

THE THREAD COLORS

In the key, the closest column of thread codes listed next to the chart symbols is the thread brand used in the design. Similar color matches are listed next.

OTHER IDEAS

This motif would look super cute stitched onto the back of a denim jacket, or onto the flap of a canvas satchel. You could also turn them into a trio of framed pictures for a crafty take on modern wall art – they're perfect for a bedroom, or how about putting them in the guest bedroom as a fun and welcoming touch?

STITCHED ONTO...
These examples are worked on 14 count white aida, 8"x8" (20x20cm) for each card. If you prefer, choose 28 count linen or other evenweave fabric.

A splash of color

Needlepoint

YOU WILL NEED

☐ Tapestry wool in a range of colors

☐ Tapestry needle – one with a large eye and a blunt tip

☐ Tapestry frame (optional – helps keep design even)

☐ Picture frame

☐ General sewing supplies, including scissors, pins, washable fabric marker, etc.

If you love fast results, you'll find needlepoint hard to resist – and it's really easy to pick up, too!

Needlepoint is a wonderfully creative stitching technique that generally involves covering an entire canvas with neat stitches in a range of styles. For the gorgeous framed piece opposite, simply combine four different stitches to create the bright, variegated look. You'll learn how to do the tent, mosaic, cushion and Gobelin stitches as well as see more pretty ideas for needlepoint.

Why not experiment with styles?

For the gorgeous framed piece here, combine four different stitches to create the bright, variegated look

Cushion stitch is fun and easy to do! Turn to page 46 to find out how.

FRAMED PICTURE

Combine cushion, tent, mosaic and Gobelin filling stitches to create a modern needlepoint sampler. Stretch your work around a piece of white mount card to finish.

GREETING CARD

Whip this cushion stitch card up in about an hour. Just pick your favorite color combinations and get going!

HOW TO...TENT STITCH
The most common and versatile stitch around

1 Bring your needle up to the front, at the bottom left of your first stitch. Take your needle back down at the top right. For each additional stitch come up at the bottom left again and back down at the top right.

2 Working in this direction is the opposite of what you're used to when cross stitching. It uses more wool, creating a thicker, sturdier finished piece. The back of your design will have a series of diagonal stitches, as above.

HOW TO...MOSAIC STITCH
Perfect for a bit of subtle texture

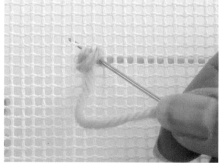

1 Work the first stitch diagonally across one block. Work the second stitch diagonally across two blocks. Work your third and final stitch diagonally across one block to finish the square.

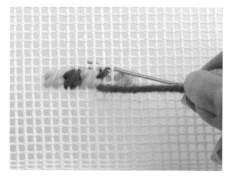

2 Repeat Step 1 for each additional square. You can choose to alternate between two colors to create a checkerboard effect, or use the same color for a more subtle textured look.

Choose from silk, cotton or metallic threads and experiment with different canvas meshes

PRETTY PATCH

This cherry design is worked in tent stitch with a mosaic stitch border. When you've finished stitching, fold the corners in, followed by the sides. Stitch or glue the folded edges before stitching to your bag or jacket.

TOP TIP

Tapestry wool works best to create the soft, filled-out look featured here. To vary the appearance of your needlepoint, choose from silk, cotton or metallic threads and experiment with different canvas meshes.

BOOKMARK

For a different effect, work Gobelin filling stitch in six strands of embroidery floss on 14 count plastic canvas. Once complete, cut to one block beyond the stitched edge.

HOW TO...
CUSHION STITCH
A diagonal stitch series – ideal for squares

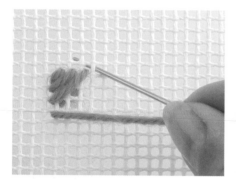

1 Begin by making a diagonal stitch over one block, make your second diagonal stitch over two blocks, your third over three and your fourth diagonal stitch over four blocks, as above.

2 Finish off the square by decreasing the diagonals until you've created a square. Work your contrasting color in the same way, but working your diagonals in the opposite direction.

BROOCH
Work this design directly onto felt using 10 count waste canvas. Switch to a sharp crewel or chenille needle to make stitching easier.

HOW TO...GOBELIN FILLING STITCH
A super-quick, high impact stitch

1 Begin by working a row of vertical stitches over six squares of your canvas. For a more compact stitch, you can work your stitches over four squares. Leave one block between each stitch.

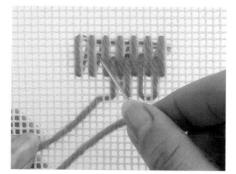

2 Work your second row of stitches between and three blocks below your first row. Continue adding each extra row in the same way, switching to a darker shade every few rows.

NEEDLEPOINT ESSENTIALS

Before you get started, ensure you have these basic bits and pieces at the ready!

MAKE A...WASTE KNOT

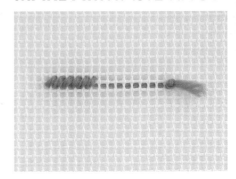

Knot one end of your wool and take it down an inch or two from your starting point. Begin stitching. Once the strand is covered in stitches, you can snip off the knot and thread end.

TAPESTRY WOOL

Tapestry wools are 4-ply and non-divisible. Stitch using just one strand in your needle. Anchor, DMC and Appleton are all high quality brands.

TAPESTRY FRAME

Tapestry frames aren't essential, but will help keep your design looking even, especially when working tighter stitches such as tent stitch.

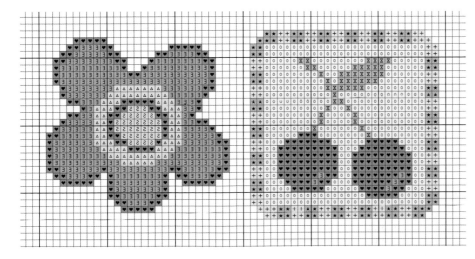

CANVAS

Try 10 count mono canvas or mono interlock canvas. Both are perfectly suitable for needlepoint, though interlock canvas is less likely to become distorted.

NEEDLES

You'll need a needle with a large eye and blunt tip – a size 18 tapestry needle is perfect.

TOP TIP

To thread your needle with tapestry wool, fold your thread end around the eye of the needle and pinch. Take this pinched loop and slide through the eye.

CHARTS FOR YOUR PROJECTS

Use spare threads from your stash to stitch up these simple motifs

Anchor tapestry wool (4-ply) used in this project

Tent stitch

8120	yellow
8216	red
8434	light pink
8436	dark pink
8986	green
9252	off-white

Mosaic stitch

+	8120	yellow
★	8806	blue

Cute crewel

Crewelwork

YOU WILL NEED

- ☐ Wool thread (or one strand of Persian thread) in various colors

- ☐ Crewel embroidery needle

- ☐ Embroidery hoop

- ☐ Ribbon for hanging loop

- ☐ General sewing supplies, including scissors, pins, washable fabric marker, etc

This striking, beautifully textured stitching technique can be used to create all kinds of stunning effects.

Even though the long stitches in crewelwork are incredibly simple to do, the effects it produces are impressively rich and textured. The technique mixes up a variety of stitches and is usually worked freehand on a canvas, but here different lengths of straight stitch are used to create pictures and patterns.

However, if you wanted to mix in other stitches too, there are a few ideas included for you to try out. There are lots of ways that crewelwork can be shown off, but in this chapter it's kept short and sweet with a stitch hoop decoration and mug cozy, as well as some ideas for embellishing, too.

Great for textures!

Crewelwork can be as simple or as intricate as you like

Even the smallest touch of crewelwork can be built to produce a 3D effect.

Trace the tree shape onto your fabric and mount centrally in your hoop. Fill in using satin stitch. Vary the lengths of your stitches to create the effect of pine needles. Finish with a few bright red chunky French knots and a running stitch border.

WORK…SATIN STITCH
A simple yet sophisticated filling stitch

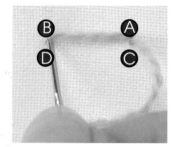

1 Begin by tracing your desired shape onto your fabric. Starting at the widest point, bring your needle up at A and back down at B. Come up again at C, directly below A, then down again at D, directly below B.

2 Continue stitching in this way for each additional stitch. For a more padded finish, first outline your shape in split stitch, then stitch over it. If you like, outline your finished shape with split stitch or backstitch.

WORK…FRENCH KNOTS
The perfect finishing touch for your design

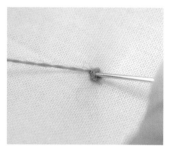

1 Bring your needle up to the front of your fabric. Hold your needle in your right hand. Use your left hand to wrap your thread around the needle. Try three wraps around the needle for a relatively chunky knot.

2 Continue holding your thread in your left hand. At the same time, pierce the fabric where you'd like the knot to be. Pull down with your left hand until the knot is on the fabric surface, then pull the needle through.

WORK…SPIDERWEB
You'll love this stitch – easy and impressive

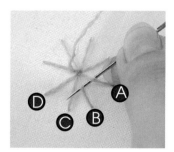
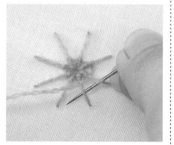

1 Trace a circle onto the reverse side of your fabric. Stitch eight evenly spaced spokes all radiating from the center point. Next, come up in through the center, weave your needle through spokes A and B and pull your thread taut.

2 For your next stitch, weave your needle through spokes B and C and pull taut. Continue for each additional stitch, going in where you've come out. Working in this way creates a thread loop, which covers the spokes.

WORK…SPLIT STITCH
Use this versatile stitch for outlining or filling

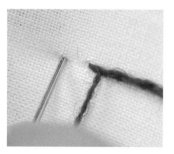

1 Begin by making a single straight stitch. You can make your stitches smaller for a neat and compact finish or slightly larger for a more open look. From the reverse, bring your needle up through the center of your first stitch.

2 Bring your needle back down again, creating a second stitch that is the same length as your first stitch. Continue in this way, neatly coming up through the center of your previous stitch, then going back down again.

MUG COZY

Cut a piece of felt to fit around your mug. To work the snowflakes, follow Step 1 of the spiderweb stitch, adding a French knot to the end of each spoke. Add blanket stitch around the edges and finish with ribbon ties at each end.

JAM JAR

Work this holly leaf design in satin stitch with chunky French knot berries. Pad the top of your jar lid with batting, stretch your fabric over the top, add a rubber band to hold in place and finish with a pretty ribbon.

COVERED BUTTONS

Felt isn't normally recommended for crewelwork, but it's just right for spiderweb stitch buttons. Go for a thin, soft felt for the best result.

SOCKS

Follow the first step of the spiderweb guide to learn how to create your designs. Instead of drawing your guidelines onto the reverse, draw on the front using a washable or fading fabric pen. Top off each spoke with a chunky French knot.

CREWEL ESSENTIALS

Before you get started, ensure you have these basic bits and pieces at the ready!

FABRIC

Linen twill is the most commonly used fabric in crewelwork. Its diagonal weave and heavy weight make it the perfect sturdy base. Thin or stretchy fabrics such as felt work well for spiderweb stitch, but aren't recommended for tighter stitches such as satin and split stitch, as the fabric will become distorted.

WOOL/PERSIAN THREAD

Crewel wool is a two-ply worsted wool, which is used singly in the needle. For high-quality crewel wool in hundreds of colors, try Appleton Brothers. It's tricky to find in the US, though, so you can also use one strand of Persian thread.

NEEDLES

You can use either a crewel needle or a chenille needle to work your designs. Both types have large eyes and sharp points, though crewel needles are a bit longer with a smaller eye. Feel free to choose the type you like best.

TEMPLATES FOR YOUR PROJECTS

Trace these outlines or create your own unique designs

Trace the templates directly onto your fabric using a pencil or a washable or fading fabric pen

HOLLY LEAVES

CHRISTMAS TREE

Busy beads
Bead embroidery

With just a handful of beads you can add sparkle to your cross stitch projects or bring a tired outfit back to life.

There's nothing like a sprinkling of beads to make a project a happy one. The tiny sparkles can be used in so many different ways, either in a contrasting color or to lift a matching color.

Learn how to add beads – from seed beads to sequins – to your projects to really make them shine. There are also some cute ideas for how to use beading to pep up garments or embellish a purse for a special occasion.

Add sparkle to projects!

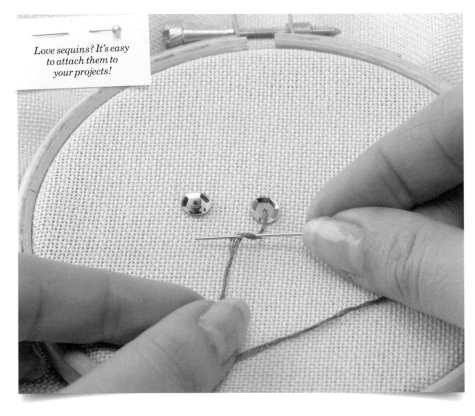

Love sequins? It's easy to attach them to your projects!

TRINKET BOX

Add a couple layers of batting to the top of your box for a padded top. Wrap the fabric tightly around the top, folding the corners, and secure with double-sided tape.

bright ideas!

♡

add sparkle to a **monogram** by stitching in some simple beads

♡

use just **one** or **two** colors for your beads for a simple and **sophisticated** look

ADD...SEED BEADS
The most common and versatile bead around

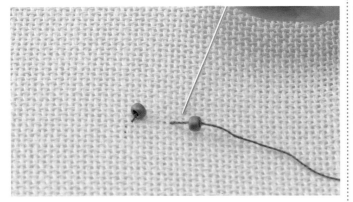

Secure your thread on the reverse and come up to the front. Slide on your bead and make a diagonal stitch across one aida block or two evenweave threads. You'll need a beading needle, which is a long, thin, flexible needle, available at craft and sewing shops.

ADD...BUGLE BEADS
Mix with seed beads for a textured look

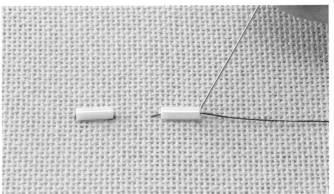

Secure your thread on the reverse and come up to the front. Slide on your bead and come back down as close to the end of the bead as you can. For extra security you can repeat. For clarity the photo shows dark thread, but you'll want to use a thread to match either your fabric or your bead.

MAKE A...
FRENCH KNOT-TOPPED SEQUIN
A quick and easy way to anchor your sequins

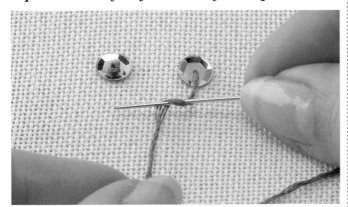

Bring your needle up through the center of your sequin. Wrap the thread around your needle a couple times, then take the needle back down through the center of the sequin to anchor in place. Try using six strands of thread for a chunky knot.

MAKE A...
BEAD-TOPPED SEQUIN
The best choice for an all-out glam finish

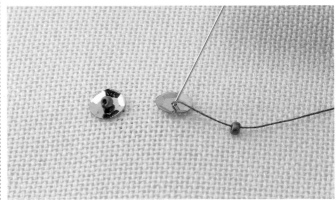

For a really sparkly finish, first bring your needle up through the sequin's center. Then thread on a seed bead and come back down through the center of your sequin to anchor. This technique is a great choice if you're not a fan of French knots.

HAIRBAND

It's official – hairbands are back! To make yours, cut out a few felt circles and layer them up, finishing with a beaded star on top. Sew or glue onto a yarn-wrapped plastic hairband and you're done.

PURSE

To create this pretty purse design, cross stitch two stars, using the chart on page 57. For the beaded star in the middle use the same chart, but replace each stitch with a seed bead instead – easy!

GLOVES

To embellish your gloves, draw on a swirly design using a fading fabric pen. Then simply fill in with embroidery floss running stitch. Add French knot or bead-topped sequins to finish the look.

SHIRT POCKET

Surely you've got a boring white shirt that's just begging to be glammed up. The trick to this look is not to overthink it – just grab a random selection of beads and start sewing.

MAKE A...PURSE
Perfect for keeping even your tiniest treasures safe

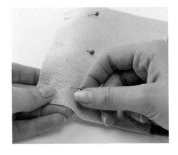   

1 Cut your stitching to ½" (1.5cm) larger than the desired finished size of the front flap. Cut some cotton fabric to the same width and twice the length. With right sides together, sew along the top edge of your stitching.

2 Open out and press the seam flat. Cut a second piece of cotton fabric to exactly the same size as the piece you've just created. You can use the same fabric as shown, or go for a contrasting patterned fabric.

3 With right sides in, pin and stitch the two pieces together, leaving an opening for turning. Turn right side out and slip stitch the opening closed. Iron to remove any wrinkles in the fabric and to create crisp seams.

4 Fold into thirds to create a pouch and top flap. Pin the sides closed. Using coordinating thread, hand stitch the sides, only sewing through the lining layers. Add a metal fastener or ribbon tie closure if you like.

CHARTS FOR YOUR PROJECTS
Use spare threads from your stash to stitch up these simple motifs

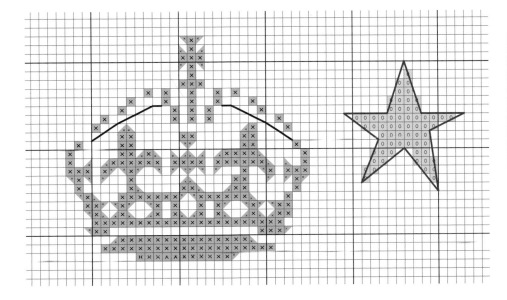

	Anchor	DMC	Madeira
Cross stitch in two strands			
✗	094	3834	0706
0	096	554	2713
Backstitch in two strands			
—	094	3834	0706 crown
Backstitch in one strand			
—	096	554	2713 star

Sparkly stitches
Metallics

Metallic threads are perfect for adding sparkle to your stitches. They're simple to work with and look so pretty too!

Everybody loves glitter, and shiny threads are perfect for making your projects really stand out. Just a few lines of simple stitching with these gorgeous threads can really enhance your work, and the metallic threads come in such a great variety of colors you are sure to find one that complements your work.

These examples use a really simple color palette for gift and party ideas, which demonstrate how effective and pretty metallic threads can look. So what are you waiting for – it's time to shine!

Make your projects sparkle!

Beeswax is a professional secret for smoother metallic stitching!

Just a few lines of simple stitching with these gorgeous threads can really make your work stand out

CAKE BAND

This cute design sparkles in DMC's Light Effects thread, and the turquoise linen adds a fresh finish. Hem the top and bottom edges of your stitching and a fabric strip. Sew your stitching in place over the fabric strip and hem the side edges to finish.

GIFT BAG

The perfect stocking filler or last-minute gift, especially when filled with chocolate truffles! The heart motif uses color blending to create a subtle sparkle, mixing one strand of Kreinik blending filament, ref 032 and two strands of turquoise embroidery floss.

WORKING... WITH METALLIC THREADS
Four top tips for easy stitching with sparkle

1 Use beeswax or a thread conditioner to help strengthen your threads and allow them to pass more easily through your fabric. Hold your thread in one hand and pull across with the other.

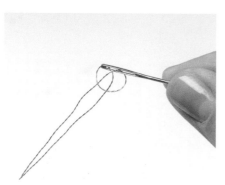

2 Stop your needle unthreading by knotting your thread at the eye of the needle. Fold your thread length in two, pass the tail ends through the eye of the needle, then pass the ends through the loop to secure.

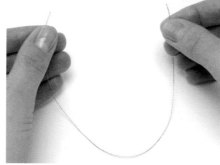

3 Metallic threads wear, fray and become tangled much more easily than embroidery flosses. One of the simplest ways to reduce this problem is to use shorter thread lengths – about 12" (30cm) is perfect.

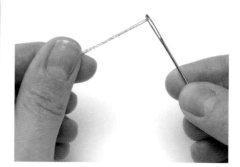

4 Try using a larger-sized tapestry needle. In addition to being easier to thread, a larger needle will help separate the holes of your aida or evenweave, reducing the amount of friction on your metallic threads.

JAR BAND

The stars have been stitched using one strand of Kreinik very fine braid. Stitch the stars randomly across the felt, hem your background fabric, machine-stitch your felt design centrally in place and hem the side edges to finish.

NAPKIN RING

Stitch by blending two metallic thread shades in the needle, and stretch over a 1½" (38mm) self-cover button. To finish simply cut two or more felt shapes, then stack and stitch onto a hemmed strip of fabric.

PLACE MAT

Waste canvas makes stitching on almost every fabric possible! This design uses 14 count waste canvas. Once you've finished, place your fabric and a piece of backing fabric right sides together. Sew all the way around, turn and slip stitch the opening closed to finish your place mat.

FOUR WAYS ...WITH METALLICS
One design – four different looks. Try them all!

DMC LIGHT EFFECTS

The first heart is stitched using two strands of DMC Light Effects threads, which are available in dozens of colors. Plus, each thread has an embroidery floss equivalent. Just remove the E from the reference code to find it.

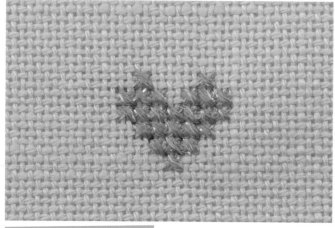

BLENDING FILAMENT

Kreinik blending filament is the thrifty choice when it comes to metallics. You can combine one strand of Kreinik blending filament ref 032 with two strands of embroidery floss to create a subtle shimmer.

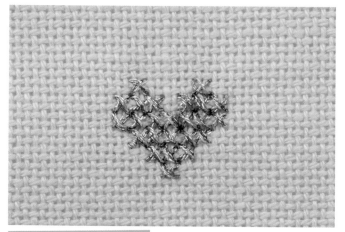

COLOR BLENDING

To create a more unusual look, combine one strand of DMC Light Effects in silver and one in turquoise. Alternatively, you can try combining one strand of metallic thread with one of embroidery floss.

KREINIK BRAID

Despite the intimidating name, Kreinik very fine braid is a breeze to use. It's smoother in texture than other metallics and non-divisible so you won't have to worry about it splitting or fraying very much.

METALLICS ESSENTIALS

Glam up your stash with a few sparkly spools

STITCH IT

You've gotten a taste of a few threads and techniques, but there are dozens more to try. If you find metallics a bit frustrating, start with Kreinik very fine braid, which is used singly in the needle, making it easier to work with. Combining embroidery floss with metallics will also make for a stress-free stitch.

CHARTS FOR YOUR PROJECTS

Stitch them on aida, evenweave or plain fabric; the choice is yours!

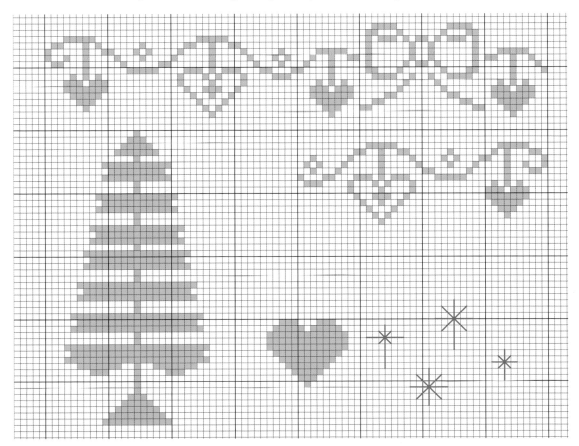

Pretty papercrafts
Stitching on paper

Take your stitching skills to the next level by stitching simple designs and adding extra embellishments on paper!

Once you've got the hang of stitching on paper, you'll open up a whole new world of crafting possibilities! As well as being able to make your own unique, handmade greetings cards, you'll be able to wrap up presents with pretty stitched gift tags and bags! The seaside theme that runs throughout this chapter is so versatile that you'll be able to use the tiny charts and templates time and time again! Learn how to personalize a notebook, create a brilliant bookmark and a make a mini magnetic photoframe from paper with simple and stunning stitched designs!

Combine stitching & papercraft!

Once you've mastered this technique, you'll start to notice lots of paper based items that could do with a touch of stitching!

Use a sharp needle or a paper piercing tool to map out your designs on paper.

MOBILE
This classic child's toy is simple to make and is really easy to personalize. Try ribbons, bows or patterned paper to get a different look. The trick to a neat finish is to keep the designs as simple as possible.

HOW TO... CROSS STITCH ON PAPER

Preparation is the key to success for this technique

   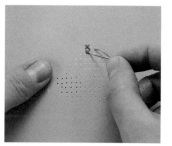

1 Begin with a scrap of aida – here a large 10 count aida is shown, but you can use 14 count aida to create slightly smaller crosses than shown here. Using your chart and a sharp pencil, draw crosses over each block to be stitched.

2 Using masking tape, attach the aida scrap on to your notebook or card. Place a few layers of felt or thick fabric underneath. Using a large needle with a sharp point, punch through only the holes to be stitched.

3 Remove the masking tape and aida swatch to reveal your design. You'll notice that on the front side the perforations are smooth while on the back they're rough and raised. Be sure to cross stitch on the front side.

4 Use a needle that's smaller than the one you punched your holes with. Stitch just as you normally would, taking care not to pull or tug as you stitch. Place your finished piece under a heavy book to flatten.

MAKE A... MOBILE

Or make a card, a bookmark or a photo frame too!

   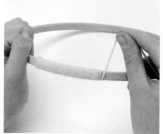

1 Use the templates provided to cut out your shapes. If you're making a mobile, you'll need a front and back for each. Use a medium to heavy weight card for best results. Thinner card may wrinkle up!

2 Place your card under felt or thick fabric and punch holes along the outside edge. The holes shown are about ¼" (5mm) apart. Add holes for the eyes and mouth too. Punch toward the reverse, to create smooth holes on the front.

3 Use running stitch for the outline, backstitch for the mouth details and French knots for eyes. For your mobile, create a front and back piece for each animal. Glue them together with a length of yarn in between.

4 Wrap yarn around a hoop. Tie four lengths of yarn, equally spaced, around the hoop. Hold up the lengths, adjusting until the hoop is level. Tie off the ends. Tie your marine animals around the hoop to finish.

BOAT CARD

This simple yet effective card works well with nearly any small motif. Just steer clear of designs containing fractionals or intricate backstitch.

PHOTO FRAME MAGNET

What better way to remember your summer vacation? Attach your picture behind the frame, followed by another piece of plain card. Finish by gluing a piece of strip magnet onto the back.

FISH BOOKMARK

Create your bookmark by stitching two fish pieces and gluing together. Punch a hole in the tail and use your leftover threads to create a colorful matching tassel.

WHALE NOTEBOOK

Choose a notebook with a relatively thin cover, to make stitching a bit easier. Your notebook's cover might curl slightly while stitching, but don't worry, an hour under a heavy book will flatten it out perfectly.

TEMPLATES FOR YOUR PROJECTS

Trace these templates, or copy and resize to your heart's content!

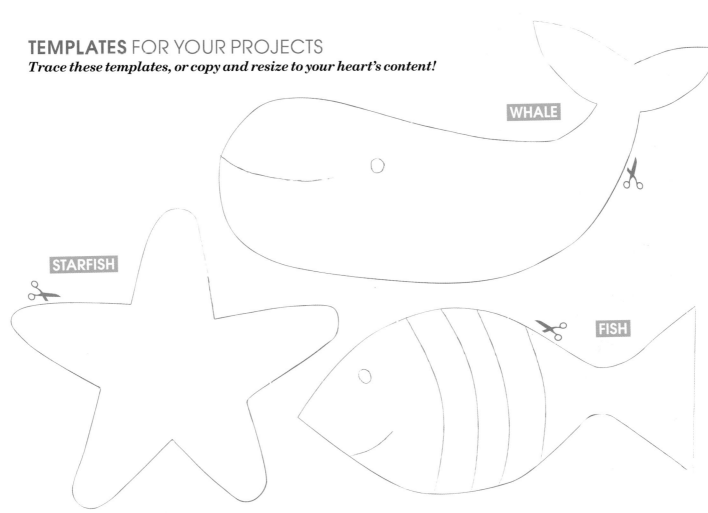

WHALE

STARFISH

FISH

CHARTS FOR YOUR PROJECTS

Use whatever spare threads you've got in your stash to stitch up these simple sea-themed motifs

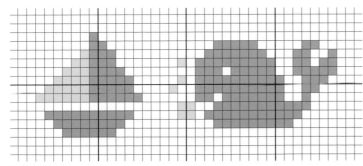

You don't have to go for a sea life theme for your projects. Try dinosaurs, flowers, pirates or butterflies for the mobile if you prefer!

Start Stitching

Embellishing

Pretty up your projects with some nifty techniques,
including stitching over patterns and appliqué

Beads & buttons

Simple embellishing

When it comes to beads and buttons, what's not to like? Here are five embellishment-inspired projects.

Once you've stitched yourself a gorgeous handmade item such as a pincushion, purse or bag, then you can have even more fun embellishing it! Cute or vintage buttons look great, as well as chunky or seed beads, depending on the look you're after. Featured here are five simple projects to help you get started with embellishing. These will make handy items for your own sewing stash or fabulous gifts for your stitching friends.

It's all in the detail!

Cute or vintage buttons look great, as well as chunky or seed beads, depending on the look you're after!

Simple stitched projects can be made even more cute with a little embellishment!

BEETLING WITH BEADS

Stitch lady bugs onto a linen band using beads for the spots. If you don't have linen band, use a strip of aida or linen and fray the edges.

BEADED BUTTERFLIES

This simple patchwork-style pincushion can be stitched and completed in an evening. Finish with a few buttons and beads and your friends will think you spent days on it!

MAKE A... BUTTERFLY PINCUSHION

Use leftover fabric scraps to create this quick gift

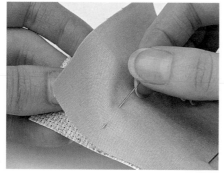

1 Stitch the motifs onto two scraps of aida and add beads. Cut the aida and two fabric pieces into equal-sized squares. Right sides in, pin and stitch one aida and one fabric piece together along one edge. Repeat on the other two.

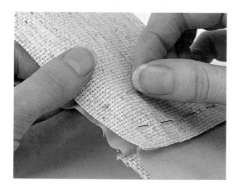

2 Use an iron to press the two pieces you created in Step 1. With the right sides together, pin and machine stitch both pieces together along one side. Line up the joins to ensure the corners come together neatly at the middle.

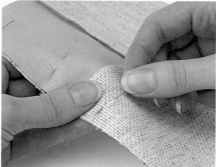

3 Once you've finished the front of your pincushion, press the seams flat. Cut a piece of backing fabric to the same size as your front piece. With right sides together pin and sew all the way around, leaving an opening for turning.

4 Turn right side out and fill as firmly as possible with stuffing. Slip stitch the opening closed. Add a button to the middle at both the front and back. Secure the button tightly to create an indent in the middle of the pincushion.

CUTE BUTTON FASTENING

Make a fun needle case by cutting two leaf shapes from red felt and two from green linen. Sandwich the felt pieces between the linen. Stitch the leaves together at the stem and add a button. Blanket stitch around the stem. Stitch the lady bug using waste canvas, and finish with beads. Add running stitch for the leaf veins.

Sparkly beads and buttons transform an old-fashioned sewing accessory into a must-have item!

ALL BUTTONED UP

Use natural linen lined with bright cotton to make this glasses case. Stitch the stalks, leaves and a tiny butterfly onto the linen and add button flowers. To make the case, line two rectangles of linen with cotton fabric and sew the rectangles together around the edge with blanket stitch.

MAKE A...
FLORAL SCISSOR KEEP
***Keep tabs on your best scissors
with this little scissor keeper***

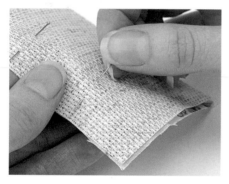

1 Cut your stitched piece and a piece of
backing fabric to the same size.
This example measures 2½"x2½"
(6x6cm). Pin and machine stitch in place,
leaving an opening for turning.

SEED BEAD TRIMS
A scissor keeper is essential for the busy, modern crafter. Add your
favorite fabric scraps and beads and you're all set.

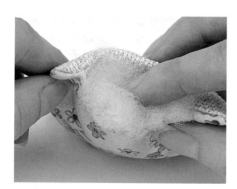

2 Fill your sachet firmly with stuffing,
using a knitting needle or scissors to
get into the corners. Slip stitch the
opening closed. If you like, add a blanket
stitch border all the way around instead.

3 Add seed beads around the outside
edge using a beading needle and
coordinating thread.

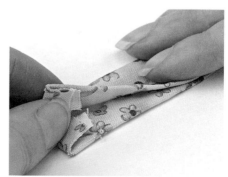

4 To create the fabric loop, cut a fabric
strip measuring 2"x6" (5x15cm).
Fold the edges in and press flat. Now fold
in half so the folded edges line up. Loop
around your scissors and stitch in place.

When it comes to beads and buttons, what's not to like? Create cute gifts with a handmade feel, perfect for your sewing friends

CHARTS FOR YOUR PROJECTS

Use these quick-to-stitch charts to create your own unique set of sewing accessories

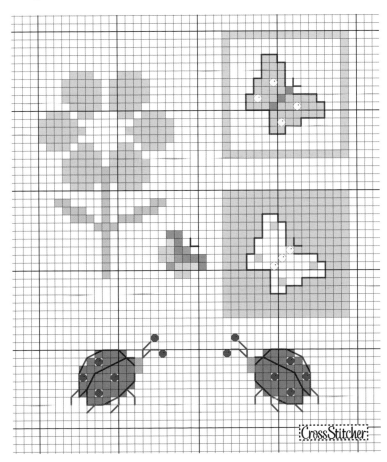

CrossStitcher

MAKE A... BUTTON JAR

Fill a Mason jar with colorful buttons, beads or threads to create the perfect adornment for your sewing table

Cut out three pieces of batting to just slightly smaller than the size of the circular lid insert. Wrap a circle of fabric tightly around the batting, secure on the bottom using double-sided tape, and insert into lid.

Upcycle fabric scraps

Simple appliqué

YOU WILL NEED

- ☐ Assorted surface embroidery linen

- ☐ Scraps of pretty fabrics

- ☐ Embroidery floss

- ☐ Embroidery needle

- ☐ Fusible webbing

- ☐ General sewing supplies, including scissors, pins, washable fabric marker, etc.

Simple appliqué is the easiest way to give your pretty fabric scraps a new lease on life

Appliqué, in easy terms, is attaching one piece of fabric to another. You can get stunning results by snipping out simple fabric shapes and stitching them to another piece of fabric. The great thing about appliqué is that all you need to get started is an embroidery needle and thread, a pair of sharp scissors, and the prettiest fabric scraps in your stash. You can appliqué with all sorts of fabrics, but cotton and felt are best for beginners. Learn how you can start using simple appliqué techniques to create a stylish teacup napkin and a cute egg cozy!

Easy embellishments!

See page 80 to find out how to use fusible webbing to help you master appliqué!

Try using a bright embroidery thread that contrasts with your fabric for a design that really stands out!

EGG COZY

No kitchen is complete without an egg cozy or two—even if you never use them! This design was inspired by a cheerful red window box filled with pansies. Before you begin, pop out to the garden and see what color combinations and shapes could inspire your design.

HOW TO...
USE FUSIBLE WEBBING

A hassle-free adhesive that every creative crafter should have in their basic workbox

1 Fusible webbing is a thin layer of adhesive attached to a thin paper backing. Carefully trace your templates from page 83 onto the smooth, paper side with a pencil.

BABY ONESIE

Embellish a plain baby onesie for a low-cost alternative to pricey store-bought items. With the help of a bit of fusible webbing and your flower templates, trace, cut and adhere the shapes together and then to the onesie itself. Add a small straight stitch around the purple flower and a running stitch around the green flower. Be sure to keep your stitches small and tight and tie off securely when finished.

2 Roughly cut around your chosen shape, leaving a 3/8" (1cm) border. Place the shape paper side up on to the reverse of your fabric. Now iron over the top to set the adhesive on the fabric.

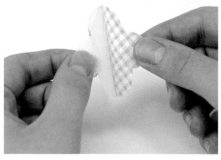

3 Cut out your shape from the fabric and remove the paper backing. Place your shape adhesive side down on your backing fabric, making sure it's in the right place.

4 Iron over the top to set it in place. Some felts can melt when ironed, so be sure to place a cloth between your felt and the iron to be safe. Now you're ready to stitch!

HEART PURSE

Cut a piece of felt to 5"x8" (13x20cm). Fold both short edges under by about ³/₈" (1cm) and machine stitch a red ribbon in place over the fold. Using fusible webbing, trace, cut and adhere your heart to one side of the felt. Stitch around the heart using running stitch. Fold your purse in half right sides together and machine stitch along the sides. Turn right side out and add a ribbon loop and button to finish.

FLOWER HAIR CLIP

Use the templates on page 83 to cut two flower shapes out of felt or cotton fabric. Attach the smaller piece to the larger using a quick running stitch or the embroidery stitch of your choice. Follow with a running stitch around the outside edge and then add a button in the middle. Secure your hair clip to the back to finish.

TEACUP NAPKIN

Using fusible webbing, trace, cut and adhere your teacup shape to your napkin. For a subtle look, use one strand of pale blue thread to work straight stitches around the shape.

bright ideas!

enlarge the little egg cozy to make a pretty teapot cozy!

appliqué works really well on **felt stockings for Christmas!** Add cute stars and snowflakes.

YOU CAN... MAKE AN EGG COZY

Stitch yourself a soft and felty cozy just like this one in no time at all

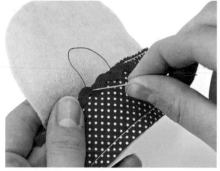

1 Use beeswax or a thread conditioner to help strengthen your threads and allow them to pass more easily through your fabric. Hold your thread in one hand and pull across with the other.

2 Place one piece of blue felt and one piece of red cotton right sides together and sew a hem along the bottom edge. Repeat this for the remaining two pieces. Once finished, open up each joined piece and press your hems flat.

3 Create your flowers by making triangular cuts in a circle of felt. Use a hole punch to cut little circles for the centers. Add a single cross stitch to each flower's center to attach it to the cozy. Finish with green backstitched stems.

4 Place your sewn pieces right sides together and sew around the shape, leaving an opening for turning on the lining side. Turn right side out and slip stitch the opening closed. Push the lining inside to create your egg cozy.

TEMPLATES FOR YOUR PROJECTS

ONESIE

ONESIE

EGG COZY

HAIR CLIP

Trace these templates on to fusible webbing for instant appliqué effects!

PURSE

TEA CUP

HAIR CLIP

In full bloom
Patterned fabric appliqué

Make the most of your pretty patterned fabrics… Just add fusible webbing and snip out the motifs to get the look!

Once you've mastered the art of simple appliqué, the next step is learning how to appliqué with patterned fabrics! You can cut out motifs from all sorts of designs, but you can't beat a fantastic floral fabric for vintage style on your homespun interior accessories and clothing. There are lots of different stitches you can use to appliqué your fabric blooms, from blanket stitch to stem stitch, so whether you're an appliqué amateur or a confident connoisseur you'll be able to add amazing motifs to your work in no time! You'll learn how to add patterned fabric to cute miniature matchboxes and pretty cake bands!

Use your favorite fabrics!

Don't worry if the thread doesn't match parts of your motif perfectly - it all adds to the homespun look!

You can use blanket stitch or a running stitch to secure your beautiful blooms!

JAM JAR COVERS

Cut a 6½" (16cm) diameter circle to create your cover. Here you see a rustic linen that will fray at the edges, but you could choose a tighter weave such as cotton if you like. Add your design to the center and embellish with a contrasting mint green blanket stitch. Finish with a rustic raffia tie.

HOW TO...APPLIQUÉ WITH PATTERNED FABRIC

It's time to grab your fabric and get snipping!

1 To begin, choose a printed cotton fabric. Fabrics that contain shapes with defined edges work best. Back your fabric with fusible webbing. Fuse the rough side of the fusible webbing to the back of your fabric using an iron.

CAKE BAND

To create this cake band, attach a 1" (2.5cm) wide aida band to a wider 2" (5cm) piece of ribbon using fusible webbing. If you'd rather, replace the aida band with a second ribbon. Finish with cut-out flowers and a few pretty beads.

2 Leave the paper fusible webbing backing in place on the reverse of your fabric and use a small, sharp pair of scissors to carefully cut out each flower or motif. A sharp pair of embroidery scissors should do the trick.

3 Remove the paper backing and arrange your cut shapes onto your base fabric until you're happy with the look. Fuse your cut fabrics in place, again using an iron. You can stop here if you'd rather not add embellishments.

4 If you like you can add a running stitch or blanket stitch around the outside edges of your shapes. Embellish with buttons or beads.

MATCHBOX

This matchbook is so sweet you'll be searching for more reasons to light candles. Add a few tiny flowers cut from a patterned fabric onto a piece of aida with a few seed beads. Back the whole piece with iron-on interfacing to stop it fraying and attach to the matchbox using double-sided tape.

HOW TO... STEM STITCH

Add stem and leaf details with this elegant stitch

Bring your thread up from the back of your fabric and make a single straight stitch. For your next stitch, come up above and just slightly overlap your previous stitch. Continue in the same way for each stitch. Stem stitch lends itself well to creating curved lines, such as stems and leaves.

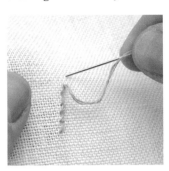

Use a sharp embroidery needle instead of a tapestry needle to work your embroidered finishing touches

LINEN NAPKINS

These napkins can be made in about 15 minutes. Simply combine a single cut-out flower with a spot of freehand stem stitching.

MAKE A...JUG COVER

Create a pretty and practical picnic essential

1 Following the patterned fabric appliqué guide, adhere a single flower to the middle of a 6½" (17cm) diameter piece of white linen. If you have a specific jug in mind, adjust this measurement to suit.

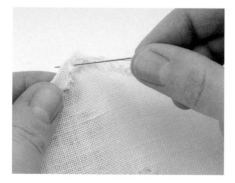

2 Fold the edges of your circle under and secure with a mint green running stitch. You'll find it easiest to work slowly, folding and stitching only a small section of the fabric circle at a time.

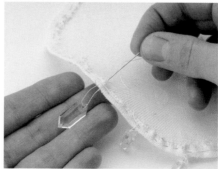

3 Using white thread, attach larger glass beads at regular intervals all the way around. These larger beads are essential as they will give your cover the weight it needs to stay in place.

4 Finish by adding small, round glass beads between the larger beads. You might want to switch to a thin beading needle to make threading your beads on to the fabric even easier.

HOW TO...BLANKET STITCH
Choose a contrasting thread for a bolder look

Secure your thread on the reverse and bring it through to the front. Take your needle back down about a quarter inch over from where you came up. Slip your needle through the loop as you go to complete the first stitch.

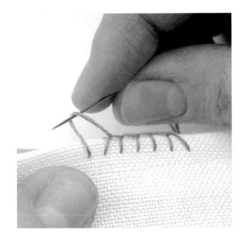

OR TRY... QUICK CARDS!
Make a quick card with even your smallest fabric scraps

Attach a few cut flowers to a piece of aida to create the look of a flower bunch. Embellish with cross stitched stems. You don't need a chart, just adjust the stems to fit your design. Fray the outer row of your aida and back onto a blank greetings card using double-sided tape.

Show the flip side
Reverse appliqué

Get to grips with this fascinating and traditional technique and start experimenting right away.

Mix and match bold, bright and beautiful fabrics to create super stylish designs using reverse appliqué. There's no fancy techniques or tools involved, so all you need is your sewing basket and the most garish fabrics in your stash – the more they clash the better! Plus, find out how you can use your newfound skill to add traditional tropical fish designs to your notebooks, keyrings and glasses case!

Traditional and trendy!

Traditional reverse appliqué uses bold contrasting colors, but you could choose a more subtle color scheme if you like

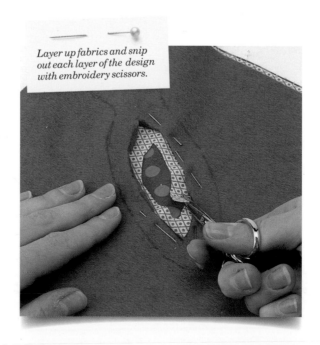

Layer up fabrics and snip out each layer of the design with embroidery scissors.

PURSE

This purse uses three layers of fabric – polka dot on top, black in the middle and orange and white stripe on the bottom. Add orange ric rac, a felt circle and a button for the eye to complete the look.

GLASSES CASE

Use four layers for this glasses case. Pink felt is on top, followed by orange, polka dot and finally black. Once you've finished the front piece, cut a second piece to the same size. Stitch the two pieces together using a running stitch or blanket stitch, leaving the mouth open.

CREATE... REVERSE APPLIQUÉ

A bit of extra time creates a beautifully tidy finish

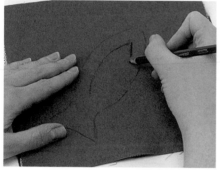

1 Layer three contrasting fabrics one on top of the other. Add a loose tacking stitch around the outside if desired to hold in place. Trace your fish shape on to the top piece using a pencil or chalk or a fabric marker.

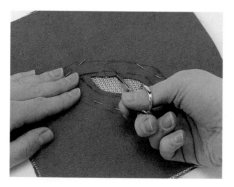

2 Using a sharp pair of scissors, cut through the top layer only. Cut around your shape about ³⁄₈" (1cm) smaller than your pencil line. Cut notches right up to the pencil line all the way around the shape for a neat finish.

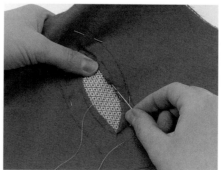

3 Fold the notches under all the way around your shape and pin. You can wait until the end to to stitch in place or stitch in place at this stage. To do so, add a slip stitch or running stitch to secure your folded edges in place.

4 Continue by cutting through to the next layer to reveal your third contrasting fabric. You can continue in this way, cutting through just one or two layers of fabric depending on which pattern you want to reveal.

BOOK COVER

Use the step-by-step guide to making a book cover on page 121 to create this cute address book cover. Attach ric rac around the edges using orange tacking stitches.

KEYRING

Cut out two felt fish shapes using the templates on page 94. Sandwich a felt or ribbon loop between the two layers at the mouth of your fish to create an instant key ring.

NOTEBOOK

For a simple finish, attach one of your appliquéd fish to the front of a notebook. Back your fabric with iron-on interfacing to keep the fabric from fraying.

bright ideas!

♡

you can cut your templates out from **all sorts of different fabrics**. Don't be afraid of mixing and matching colors, textures and styles!

TEMPLATES FOR YOUR FISH

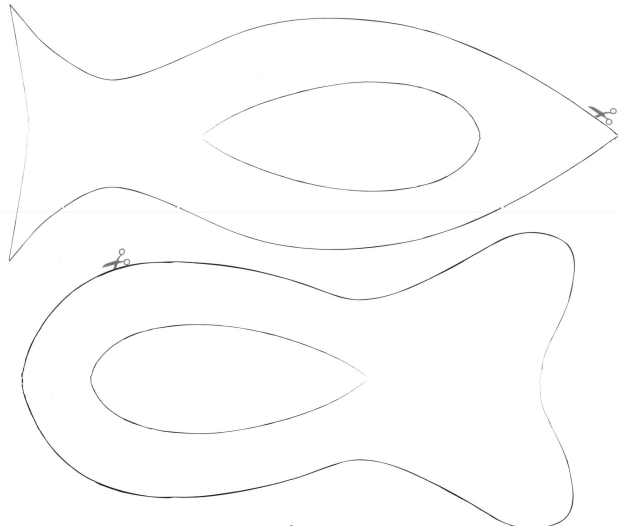

To create the fish bone effect, start with a vertical line of stitches. Work short diagonal lines coming off the vertical line to create the look

GET THRIFTY

Revive an old holey shirt with reverse appliqué. Simply draw and cut out a shape around the hole and seal the edges with fray stop. Place a piece of fabric underneath and handstitch in place.

Bright & beautiful
Patterned fabric embroidery

Use your cross stitch skills on a whole new canvas, using patterned fabrics as inspiration for stitches and beading.

Embroidery on any fabric gives a beautiful effect, but are you looking for something a bit different than the usual aida or evenweave? Well, if you're short on training time, then instead of learning a totally new technique why not put your cross stitch skills to use in a totally new way? Just swap your tapestry needle for a sharp embroidery needle and your aida for some gorgeous patterned fabrics, and start stitching. Polka dots large and small are the perfect starting point. Once you get going, beads and French knots will add even more appeal.

Mix and match your scraps!

3 WAYS... CROSS STITCH ON FABRIC
Here are just a few ideas to get your creative juices flowing...

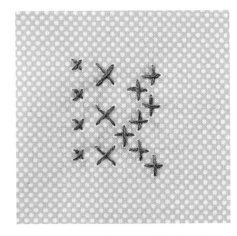

1 For fabrics with tiny polka dots, just pretend each dot is an aida hole and get stitching in any size or direction!

2 Work across just one gingham square or several, as shown here, to create a more varied effect.

3 This technique is the quickest and easiest way to add some personality to a simple fabric.

bright ideas!
♡
concentrate on **one detail**, such as a flower, for a subtle pop of color
♡
introduce **metallic threads** for a hint of **sparkle** and glamor!

BEADED BIRD CUSHION

For this project, add French knots around some birds and beads around others. To finish the cushion, cut another piece of fabric for the backing. Right sides in, sew, leaving an opening for turning. Turn, stuff and slip stitch closed.

FABRIC COASTERS

These coasters are ideal for an ice cold glass of lemonade. Assemble the coaster before adding your stitches to create a lovely quilted effect.

FABRIC POUCH

Even if you don't learn a single new stitch, you can still create a mini-masterpiece. Work this fabric pouch using nothing but backstitch. Just stitch some details and leave others plain to create an interesting contrast.

ZIPPER PURSE

Work this design in a combination of backstitch and stem stitch, using four strands to give a nice strong look. The seeds in the center of the flower have been worked using simple single chain stitches.

HOW TO... STEM STITCH

This popular outlining stitch is ideal for flower stems, but can be used for other things too

 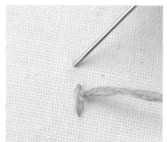 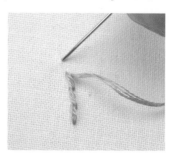 

1 Begin with a single straight stitch, as shown. This stem stitch is worked in four strands, but the choice is yours. You can also experiment with thin wools and pearl cotton.

2 For your next stitch, come up from the back to the front just to the right of your previous stitch. Then take your needle back down again. Make sure that each stitch is the same length.

3 Continue in the same way for each stitch, making sure you're always coming up on the same side. For example, if you start by coming up to the right, each additional stitch should too.

4 Stem stitch can be used for nearly anything that comes to mind, but it's especially good for outlining curved shapes such as flowers, vines and, of course, for stitching plant stems!

HOW TO... CHAIN STITCH

In this technique, a series of looped stitches produce a chain-like pattern

   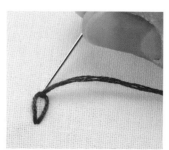

1 Using a sharp embroidery needle, bring your needle up to the surface of your fabric. Come back down through the exact same hole. Instead of pulling all the way through, leave a small loop on the front of your fabric.

2 Bring your needle back up to the surface, about a quarter inch away, catching your needle in the loop as you go. Carefully pull your thread until the loop is formed, taking care not to tug too tightly.

3 For the next loop, repeat the process by coming back down through the same hole and leaving a small loop on the front of your fabric. Be sure to keep each additional loop the same size as your first loop.

4 To close the chain, make a small tacking stitch around your loop. For the single chain stitches like in the cushion and purse featured, stitch just one loop, then make a small tacking stitch to secure before moving on to the next.

MAKE...
FABRIC COASTERS

Give your home a handmade feel with these quick and simple quilted coasters

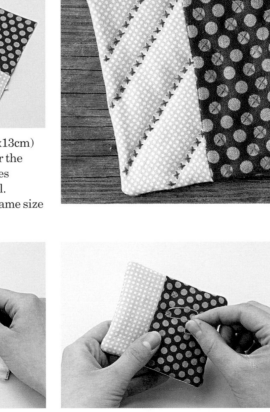

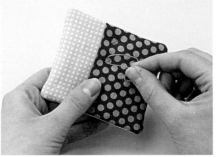

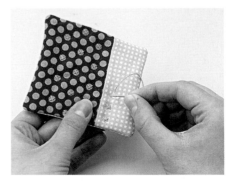

1 You'll need two 5½"x5½" (13x13cm) pieces of patterned fabric. For the front piece, you can sew two pieces together, to give a patchwork feel. Cut two pieces of batting to the same size as well.

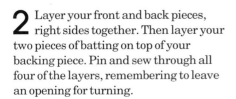

2 Layer your front and back pieces, right sides together. Then layer your two pieces of batting on top of your backing piece. Pin and sew through all four of the layers, remembering to leave an opening for turning.

3 Turn your coaster right sides out and slip stitch the opening closed. Begin adding the cross stitches on to your coaster. For a bold look, go for four strands of a bright, clashy shade, such as orange.

4 Continue adding your cross stitches across the whole of your coaster, using different colors as you wish. As you stitch you'll create a quilted effect. The more stitches you add, the more pronounced this will be.

HOW TO... SPLIT STITCH

This versatile stitch can be used for outlining as well as filling in outlined shapes

1 Begin by making a single straight stitch. You might find shorter stitches will give you a neater finish than slightly longer ones, but it's up to you. Experiment to find out what length works for you.

PATCHWORK BEADED CUSHION
Create a patchwork effect by stitching four contrasting fabric squares together. You'll find it easiest to add your embellishments before sewing the pieces together.

2 Come up through the middle of your first stitch to split it. Because the threads are being split, only divisible threads such as embroidery thread should be used, so it's best to steer clear of pearl cotton, for example.

3 Now come back down through your fabric again, thus creating a second stitch. Be sure that each subsequent stitch is the same length as the first, otherwise you'll get an uneven finish.

4 Continue each stitch in the same way. Split stitch is great for outlining, but can be used for filling in solid areas as well. Stitch your rows of split stitch one right next to the other to create the effect.

CHOOSING FABRICS

Try an unrestrained color palette inspired by your choice of fabrics, adding contrasting thread shades for further impact. Whether you go bold or subdued, you'll get the best results from your projects by choosing fabrics in varying shades and pattern sizes.

HOW TO... SATIN STITCH

Use this series of straight stitches to cover whole areas of your background fabric

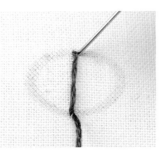

1 Start at the widest point of the shape that you'd like to fill in. Bring your needle up at the bottom and back up at the top of the shape, creating a vertical line. This example uses four strands of floss.

2 For your next stitch, come up at the bottom again, and back down at the top, directly next to your first stitch. Be sure you're always coming up at the bottom and going back down at the top.

3 Continue stitching in this way for each additional stitch, until you've filled in the whole area. Your stitches should lie neatly next to each other without any obvious gaps and without any overlapping.

4 Satin stitch can be difficult to master, but practice makes perfect. Plus, if you're not totally happy with the finished result, you can outline the edges to neaten things up, as shown.

Wrapped in ribbon

Ribbon flowers

Ribbon flowers look pretty wherever they bloom and they're simple to do, too! Be as flamboyant as you like.

One of the best things about ribbon is how versatile it is, from practical uses to pretty embellishments; it's one thing you can never have too much of. And with so many patterns and colors to choose from, it's easy to soon create a veritable garden full of gorgeous ribbon flowers to add as embellishments to your favorite jackets or your comfiest cushions.

Ribbon flowers also look great on gifts, so try them on a greeting card or even a candle holder to give away as a special present.

Quick and easy!

It's easy to create a veritable garden full of ribbon flowers to add as embellishments to your favorite jackets or your comfiest cushions

Don't be shy of pattern! Read on to find out how to make your blooms.

CUSHION

Whether you want to make a cushion from scratch or add a splash of color to an old favorite, these ribbon flowers are just the thing. You can even create them to suit the color scheme of the room.

MAKE...PRETTY RIBBON FLOWERS

Choose ribbons in a variety of colors and patterns for an eye-catching look

SHOPPING BAG

If your favorite shopping bag is looking in need of a little TLC, give it a new lease on life with a coordinating corsage. This one uses grosgrain ribbon, which has a slight texture.

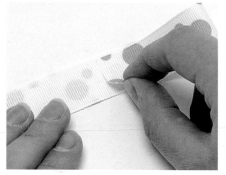

1 Once you've selected your ribbon, you'll need to cut it to length. These flowers measure about 4" (10cm) in diameter, so cut each length to measure about 8" (20cm). Now fold one end to the center and secure with a couple of stitches.

2 The next step is to fold the second ribbon end towards the center, overlapping with the first ribbon end by about ¼" (0.5cm). Stitch securely, and then repeat to create each petal. You'll need at least three or four petals.

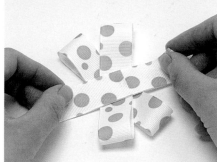

3 Now start to assemble by placing each petal together, fanning each one to create the floral shape. Once you're happy, stitch together – a thimble will help as you'll be stitching through quite a few layers of ribbon.

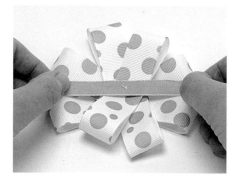

4 Once this is complete, start to create additional petals using contrasting ribbons, as shown here. Finish by adding a button to the center, to cover your tacking stitches. Add a safety pin or brooch clip to create a corsage.

Start Stitching

CORSAGE

The perfect accessory for a summer wedding, girls' night out or simply to brighten up a favorite jacket! Once the flower is assembled, disguise the ribbon ends with a couple of buttons, and secure a brooch clasp on the reverse.

PRETTY CARD

Say it with flowers! This gift card is really easy to make – each petal is made individually using the petal turnover technique (see page 106) and then arranged together. The flower's center uses the gathered flower technique.

TOP TIP

Ribbons always look great at weddings from simple bows tied around jars to an added flourish for table centerpieces. Brides can also have a special bouquet to keep forever with flowers made from silk ribbon and pearly buttons. Make the flowers from broad strips of luxuriant ribbon and attach to wire; you can then wrap around the 'stalks' with more ribbon.

CANDLE HOLDER

The uses for this are endless! Other ideas could include decorating a vase, wrapping around a table napkin or how about brightening up your utensils pot? Each petal turnover is made individually. You may find using a thimble will save your fingers when stitching together!

THREE TOP TIPS...
RIBBON FLOWERS

Just a few pointers to help you create your masterpieces!

1 Use a coordinating thread to secure your ribbon just in case your stitches are still on show after you've added the central button. If you've got a patterned ribbon, just choose the most prominent color.

2 Use pinking shears to cut the ribbon to prevent fraying, or alternatively you can add a dab of glue to your cut ends – this will do the trick too.

3 Choose a selection of different ribbon widths and textures to see which work well. Grosgrain ribbons hold their shape well, whereas some woven cotton and silk ribbons are less rigid and can be more difficult to work with.

MAKE A...PETAL TURNOVER

Use this technique when you've got a ribbon with a pattern printed on just one side

1 Cut a ribbon length measuring about 4" (10cm). Now hold the ribbon horizontally, using both hands.

2 Place the two ribbon-ends on top of each other, right side up, and stitch together where they meet.

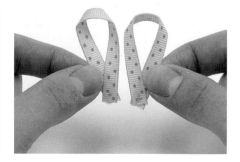

3 This turnover can be used either way, as shown here, to create two subtly different effects.

MAKE A...GATHERED FLOWER
These look great on their own or as the center of a larger flower

1 Ribbons with a width of about ½" (1.5cm) work best for this technique. Cut your ribbon to measure about 4" (10cm). Fold one end to the reverse and secure with your tacking thread.

2 Now work a running stitch along one edge of the ribbon using even stitches of about ¼" (0.5cm) in length. Be sure to choose a coordinating colored thread to work your running stitch.

3 Once you've finished working the running stitch, carefully pull your thread end to create the pleated effect, until the ribbon curls back in on itself. You will now have a circular shape.

4 Secure this ribbon end by stitching in place using the excess of the thread you used to create the running stitch. A couple of small tacking stitches will be enough to hold it in place.

You probably already have a stash of ribbons and buttons at home. Even the smallest ribbon scrap could be made into a flower

Fabulous felt!

Felt tags

YOU WILL NEED

☐ Scrap felt, various colors

☐ Embroidery thread, various colors

☐ Embroidery needle

☐ Ribbon scraps, various colors

☐ General sewing supplies, including scissors, pins, washable fabric marker, etc

Using simple techniques, create beautiful gift tags that will be treasured and re-used time after time.

Try something different the next time you give a gift, to make it feel really special. These tiny felt tags give a cute handmade touch, and they couldn't be simpler to put together. Even better, they will last for years to come if the recipients treat them with a little bit of TLC. They could even pass on the crafty love by reusing them for their presents. But the best bit is they are the perfect thing for using up scraps of felt in your craft stash!

You'll learn how to make bright and beautiful circular tags, as well as a cute heart-shaped tag for special friends.

Raid your craft stash for scraps!

These tiny felt tags give a cute handmade touch, and they couldn't be simpler to put together

Felt is so easy to work with and needs no special tools— perfect for a quick make!

TRIO OF CIRCLES

Even thick felt is a breeze to stitch on. Using a sharp embroidery needle and waste canvas, stitch a heart in the center of each felt circle. Complete the look with simple brown paper and contrasting cotton ribbons.

TRIPLE LAYERED TAG
Turn a felt circle into a jumbo gift tag by adding a metal eyelet. Layer up smaller felt shapes, adding contrasting running stitches to each piece.

MAKE A... TAG
A simple yet thoughtful personalized gift

1 Add your running stitch to the first piece of felt. For the second, add your running stitch through both layers to secure. Finish by attaching a small heart shape with a single large cross stitch.

2 Mark out where you'd like to place your eyelet at the top of your tag. Take a pair of sharp embroidery scissors and carefully create a hole in the felt that will be large enough to fit your metal eyelet.

3 Pop your metal eyelet through the hole you have just created. If you'd prefer, you can make these stages much quicker and easier by investing in a tool to fit the eyelet for you (see next step).

4 To use a traditional eyelet setter, turn to the reverse, holding your eyelet in place. Place your setter over the back of the eyelet and tap with a hammer. Or, use an eyelet setter tool like a Crop-A-Dile™ (see image above) to set your eyelet.

NAME TAG

This tag can be used again and again by replacing the card pieces. Once you've finished stitching, back with a second piece of felt to add stability and secure with a running stitch.

PINK BAUBLE TAG

Create a chunky effect by stitching each X twice as big as normal. You can copy this simple pattern or try something a bit more complicated.

PAPER AND FELT TAG

For a tag you can make in minutes, add a contrasting running stitch to a felt heart, then top with a second heart shape. Attach to a plain brown gift tag using fabric glue or double-sided tape.

GIFT TAG CHARTS

Here are just a few charts to get you started. You can also copy your favorite fonts, if you'd like to personalize your gift tags with a monogram.

EMBROIDERY FLOSS

Use three or four strands of floss, to make sure your stitching stands out against the bold felt.

MATERIALS

FELT

Try thick hand dyed wool felt to give your tags a rustic handmade finish.

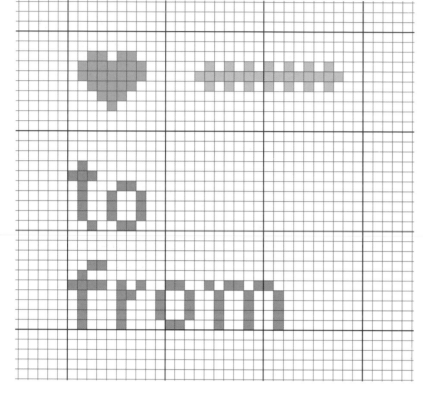

COTTON RIBBON

Check out the beautiful matte finish of woven cotton ribbons.

Start Stitching

Let's celebrate!

Stitched party treats

From mini flags to treat bags, let your favorite hobby take center stage at your next party.

The perfect handmade party needs perfect handmade decorations to keep the celebrations special. These unique touches add stacks of character and flair to the occasion and can be tailored to fit the theme of your party.

In this chapter, learn to make cute cross-stitched flags to top sandwiches and cupcakes, as well as bunting cards, ruched fabric brooches and, for when the celebrations continue into the wee hours, jar lanterns with tiny bunting detail. It's time to party!

Great for using up scraps!

YOU WILL NEED

- ☐ Embroidery floss
- ☐ Embroidery needles
- ☐ Scrap paper in various colors
- ☐ Scrap fabric in various colors
- ☐ Ribbon
- ☐ Cocktail sticks
- ☐ Jam jars
- ☐ Baker's twine
- ☐ General sewing supplies, including scissors, pins, washable fabric marker, etc.

These unique handmade touches will add stacks of character and flair to your special celebrations

Simple ruched fabric transforms into a beautiful brooch.

FABRIC TREAT BAGS

These fabric treat bags can be used again and again – if you can keep your guests from taking them home, of course. Use scraps of fabric you already have, mixing and matching to create a truly unique effect.

bright ideas!

♡

mix up **plain with patterned** to make your decorations even more fun

♡

stitch pretty detail onto ribbon to tie around **jars filled with goodies**

MAKE...
FABRIC TREAT BAGS

The perfect quick and easy stash-buster – any scrap will do!

1 Trim four pieces of fabric to 5"x7" (12x18cm). Stitch your design onto one of the pieces using waste or soluble canvas. The bottom of your design should be about 1¾" (4.5cm) from the bottom fabric edge.

BUNTING CARD

Stitch your letters directly onto fabric scraps. No chart required – just go for it, free-hand! Then simply cut to size and attach to baker's twine. Finish by sticking the entire string of bunting to your card front.

2 With right sides in, machine sew your stitched piece and a second fabric piece together, along the top edge only. Repeat this process for your remaining two patterned fabric pieces.

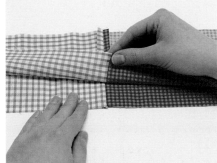

3 Open both sets of sewn pieces out and press the seams. Right sides in, pin and sew around the outside edge, leaving an opening for turning and lining up the seams at the middle.

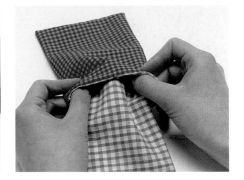

4 Turn right sides out, and carefully push out the corners with a pair of scissors. Slip stitch the opening closed. Push the lining inside. Fill with goodies and tie with baker's twine.

It's easier to stitch your heart motifs onto a larger piece of fabric, then cut out each flag afterwards

JAR LANTERN

It's easiest to stitch your heart motifs on a larger piece of fabric. Then cut out and glue each bunting piece to a length of baker's twine using fabric glue. Once dry, loosely tie around your jar, add a tea light and enjoy.

TOP TIP

Snip small pieces of plastic canvas into flag shapes and stitch using bright colorfast threads to make cupcake toppers – this means they can be gently rinsed and reused for the next big birthday party! Plastic canvas is also useful for creating stitched badges to pop in a party bag for all your guests. And, if you're feeling really adventurous, you can make 3D shapes to use as a base for place card holders.

MINI FLAGS

Dress up everything from cupcakes to cucumber sandwiches. Use waste canvas to stitch your heart onto felt, then back with a second felt piece using fabric glue. Cut into a flag shape and attach to a bamboo skewer.

BROOCH

No party hostess would be complete without a bright and bold party brooch. This one is made by layering felt pieces on top of a fabric rosette and finishing with gingham ribbon. See below to learn how to make yours.

MAKE A... BROOCH

No party hostess should be without this fabulous accessory!

1 Stitch your heart onto a piece of felt using waste canvas or soluble canvas. Once dry, trim around the shape. Cut a second heart shape slightly larger than the first. Attach the two hearts together using fabric glue.

2 Create a fabric rosette by adding a running stitch around the outside edge of a circle of patterned fabric. Leave both thread ends unsecured. The fabric circle will need to have a diameter of approximately 4½" (11cm).

3 Slowly pull the two thread ends until the fabric edges meet at the center. Thread your needle with the two thread ends and stitch back and forth through the center of the rosette a few times to secure in place.

4 Attach your heart to the center of the rosette using fabric glue. Attach two lengths of gingham ribbon to the back, using a small amount of fabric glue to secure the cut ends. Finish by attaching a brooch back.

CHARTS FOR YOUR PROJECTS

The best way to use up all your leftover threads, whatever colors you have!

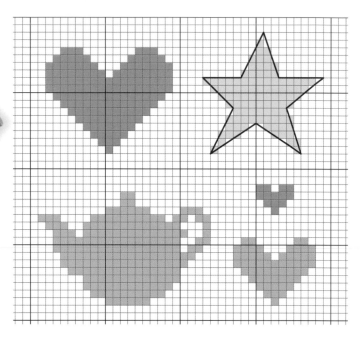

FABRIC STITCHING

These cross stitch party projects are worked using three strands to make sure the colors really pop. Instead of the usual tapestry needle, go for a sharp embroidery needle, as this will make piercing through the fabric or felt much easier.

Lovely letters
Monograms

This traditional lettering technique can be used to add personal touches to gifts and household items.

From delicately embroidered handkerchiefs to bold woodblock style cushions and throws, simple-yet-versatile monograms can transform a wide range of items. Whether your style is traditional, feminine or contemporary, you'll learn how to create smart, simple items that are sure to stand the test of time.

Choose from one of these cute monogrammed projects, which include a book cover and Oxford sachet, to give away as a special gift or keep all to yourself. But, for now, it's time to get started with a cozy hot water bottle cover.

A quick and easy gift!

Turn to page 122 to make a pretty Oxford sachet for your linen.

A timeless and classic design that will make your gifts look extra special with an added personal touch

CUTE HOT WATER BOTTLE COVER

Everything is better in miniature – including this cozy hot water bottle cover. Make your own cover or dress up a plain one using two simple felt circles.

MAKE A... SIMPLE BOOK COVER
A simple yet thoughtful personalized gift

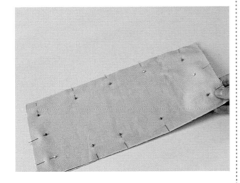

1 Cut two pieces of fabric so it is approximately 2" (5cm) bigger than the size of your open book. Cross stitch your design on the right hand section of one of the fabric pieces. Sew together, and turn right sides out.

2 Make folds at approximately 3¼" (8cm) on each side, to create pockets for sliding the book covers in. Pin the fabric in place and hand sew the top and bottom of each pocket, making sure to sew through the lining fabric only.

BOOK COVER
Transform a simple address book into a personalized gift that anyone on your list would love. Try a pale blue linen, to add that 'imperfect' element to the finish.

USING... WASTE CANVAS
Use this to stitch on a wide range of fabrics

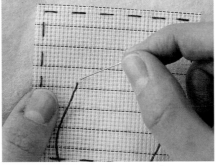

1 Tack or pin your waste canvas in place before you begin stitching. Just like when stitching on evenweave, you'll need to stitch over two waste canvas threads as opposed to a single block.

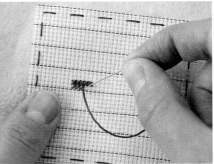

2 Continue stitching. Unlike soluble canvas, you can also stitch whole stitches. Once finished, soak your design in water to loosen the threads. Then remove each thread using tweezers.

MAKE AN...
OXFORD SACHET
Keep your linens fresh and breezy with this easy project

1 Cut your stitching to 4½"x4½" (11x11cm). Cut your backing fabric to the same size. With right sides in, sew all the way around. Cut a small x in the center of your backing. Turn right sides out, push out the corners and press the edges.

2 Add a running stitch border in a contrasting color, ³⁄₈" (1cm) from the edge. Fill with stuffing and sew the cut opening closed. Cover up the opening with a small patch of patterned fabric, securing with craft glue or fusible webbing.

OXFORD SACHETS
Thanks to a few savvy time-saving techniques, these mini sachets are easier than ever to whip up. Fill with lavender and pop in your wardrobe – classy!

USING... SOLUBLE CANVAS
For an easier, aida-like canvas, try soluble

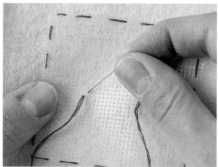

1 If you're working a design that doesn't contain fractional stitches, DMC soluble canvas may be easier to work with. Hand tack or pin your canvas in place before you begin your stitching.

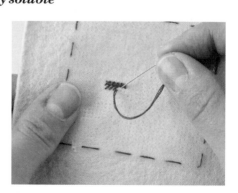

2 Continue stitching as you would on aida. Once finished, soak in warm water to dissolve the canvas. You may need to give your fabric a second soak to make sure the canvas has fully dissolved.

ALPHABET CHARTS

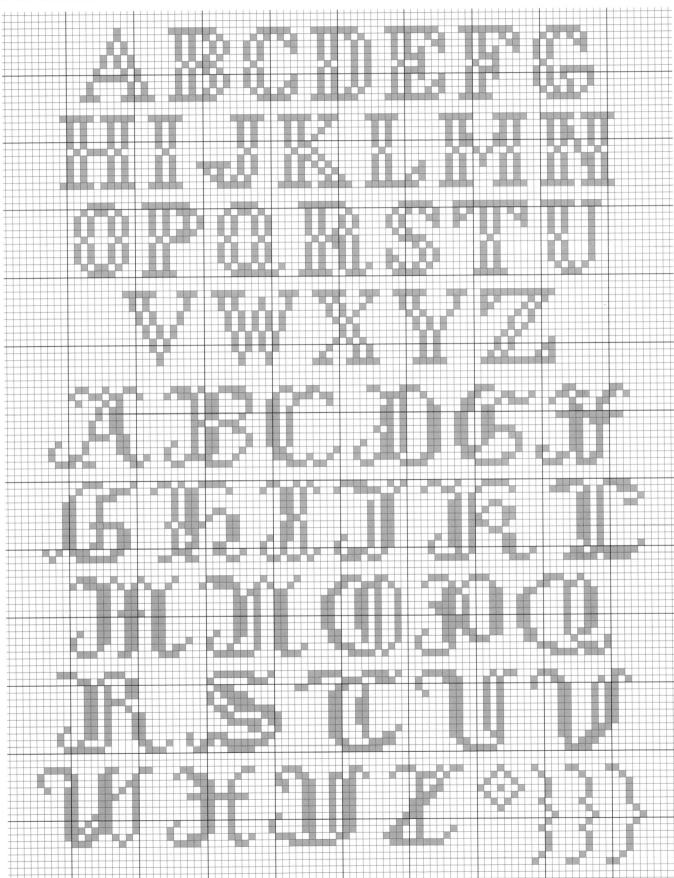

Perfect circles
Framing with hoops

This technique for displaying your work is simple to create. Combine with vintage florals for an on-trend look.

Sometimes your cross-stitch projects demand to be seen by the world, and the best way to do this is by framing them and hanging them on the wall for all to admire. And what better frame than an embroidery hoop!

Here you'll learn some simple ways to tweak this basic idea, so you can create a look that's fun and unique to you and your project. Start by learning the best way to mount your finished piece, as well as some fabulous ideas for your frames.

Perfect for an on-trend gift!

HOW TO...MOUNT YOUR WORK
Get a professional and stylish finish in just minutes

1 Trim your stitching and a piece of backing fabric into a circle that's slightly larger than your hoop. Iron both pieces until perfectly smooth. You can also use spray starch if you have some to hand, for added smoothness.

2 Place the inside hoop beneath your work and the outer hoop on top. Center and press over your work. If necessary, pull your fabric edges until the front is taut and smooth. Tighten the screw as much as you can.

3 Turn your stitching to the reverse and cut a piece of felt to fit the inside of the inner circle. Place the felt inside the circle. You can use a bit of glue to keep it in place. Adding felt will keep your work looking fresh.

4 Using a glue gun or double-sided tape, begin attaching the first layer of fabric, pulling taut as you go. Repeat for the second layer. Cut a second felt circle to fit over the back of your hoop and secure in place to finish.

bright ideas!

mix and match different size hoops to display together

stitch **simple messages**, such as 'home sweet home' onto the linen for a warm **welcoming vibe**

PATTERNED FABRIC

Instead of using evenweave or aida, stitch a few smaller designs directly onto some vintage fabric using waste or soluble canvas.

RIBBON-WRAPPED

Wrap a hoop in dusky pink ribbon for a perfectly polished look. You can also try using yarn or thin strips of your favorite fabric.

THE VINTAGE EFFECT

Creating a hoop that looks like it's been discovered in the back of an antique shop is simple. In fact it's easier than doing a traditional paint job as imperfections are actively encouraged!

FINISH WITH A BOW

For that extra-special finishing touch, add a pretty bow to the top of your hoop. Try a rustic linen ribbon. Trim the ends and dab the cut edges with glue to prevent them fraying.

CHARTS FOR YOUR PROJECTS

This rose is stitched on a 19"x19" (48x48cm) piece of 28 count antique white linen; the two smaller designs use 14 count waste canvas.

	DMC	Anchor	Madeira			DMC	Anchor	Madeira
Cross stitch in two strands					**Cross stitch in two strands**			
♥	224	893	0813		♥	3350	077	0603
▸◂	469	267	1503		@	3364	261	1603
#	471	266	1501		0	3774	778	0306
𝄞	562	210	1206		△	3813	875	1701
□	611	898	2107		X	3816	876	1703
∩	754	1012	0305		Ɜ	3833	1023	0609
=	831	277	2201					

More Great Books from Design Originals

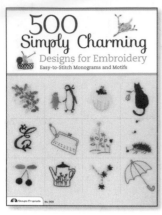

**500 Simply Charming
Designs for Embroidery**
ISBN 978-1-57421-509-0 **$14.99**
DO5430

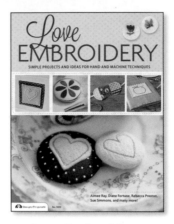

Love Embroidery
ISBN 978-1-57421-612-7 **$17.99**
DO5302

Sew Me! Sewing Basics
ISBN 978-1-57421-423-9 **$19.99**
DO5394

Sew Me! Sewing Home Decor
ISBN 978-1-57421-504-5 **$14.99**
DO5425

Sewing Pretty Little Things
ISBN 978-1-57421-611-0 **$19.99**
DO5301

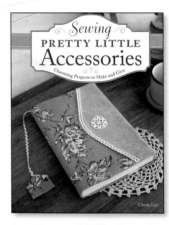

Sewing Pretty Little Accessories
ISBN 978-1-57421-861-9 **$19.99**
DO5435

**Handmade Leather
Bags & Accessories**
ISBN 978-1-57421-716-2 **$19.99**
DO5036

Handmade for Christmas
ISBN 978-1-57421-508-3 **$14.99**
DO5429

Felt from the Heart
ISBN 978-1-57421-365-2 **$9.99**
DO3488

Look for These Books at Your Local Bookstore or Specialty Retailer or at *www.D-Originals.com*